Burn Anger
Before
Anger Burns You

BOOKS AND BOOKLETS
by J. P. Vaswani

From Hell to Heaven
Tear-Drops
Pictures and Parables
Glimpses
Whispers
A Child of God
You Are Not Alone!
A Day with Dadaji
The Kingdom of Krishna
From Darkness Into Light
A Mystic of Modern India
Doors of Heaven
Love and Laugh!
The Story of a Simple Man
Beloved Dadaji
Conversations with Dadaji
Feast of Love
Shanti Speaks
Glimpses Into Great Lives
Education: What India Needs
Life After Death
How to Have Real Fun Out of Life and other Talks
Notes from the Master's Lute
Chitra Darshan (Hindi)
Stories for Meditation
Heaven Can Wait
Little Lamps
How to Overcome Tensions
Life is a Love-Story
Daily Appointment With God
Begin the Day with God
Prophets and Patriots
You can Be a Smile Millionaire
Temple Flowers
How to Meditate
Prayers of a Pilgrim
Teach Me to Pray
The Simple Way
Invest in the Child
The Holy Man of Hyderabad
I Have Need of You
Ticket To Heaven
I Luv U, God!
101 Stories For You And Me
Joy, Peace Pills
Tips For Teenagers
Why Do Good People Suffer?

Burn Anger
Before
Anger Burns You

By
J. P. Vaswani

GITA PUBLISHING HOUSE

Publishers of books and journals – of interest to those who believe that Knowledge is one, that Sages and Seers *(Rishis)* are the true Leaders of civilisation, that, alike in East and West, they have been the true benefactors of the Race who have lighted the way forward with *Bodhi,* the Wisdom of the Heart.

First Edition: 1992
Second Edition: 1996
Third Edition
(5,000 Copies): 1998

Printed by:

Mehta Offset Pvt. Ltd.,
A-16, Naraina II,
New Delhi - 110 028 (India)

Published by:

P. N. Manchandya
Gita Publishing House,
10, Sadhu Vaswani Path,
Pune-411001 (India).

PUBLISHERS' NOTE

Anger is an eroding emotion. It is a natural, but negative emotional response to stress or opposition. If we do not deal with it firmly and positively, it will keep on destroying our inner selves.

This beautifully produced book is a compilation of a few talks given by Dada J. P. Vaswani. It tells us how to deal with anger— the No. 1 enemy of our individual peace —and the negative emotions that go with it.

In his clear, inimitable style, Dada Vaswani presents his logical and practical suggestions to help us in understanding, controlling and dealing with anger. He tells us how to overcome anger by forgiveness, understanding and laughter. He provides answers to our most oft-asked queries about anger with the insight that combines the wisdom of the best Indian traditions with the well-proven and scientific approach of western thinkers and philosophers. The balanced and sensible approach prescribed by Dada Vaswani does not merely generate physical benefits but mental and spiritual health as well.

Here is a book of great value. It is a self-help book which presents practical guidelines to encourage us to be the persons we were really meant to be.

An excellent book for everyone of us.

CONTENTS

Burn
Anger
Before
Anger Burns You!

Anger is more destructive than fire, more disastrous than an earthquake.

In anger, individuals fight each other with dire consequences.

In anger, nations fight each other and thousands of young, precious, promising lives are lost.

Anger can be controlled!

CHAPTER ONE

All Over A Naya Paisa!*

This happened in Delhi, several years ago, when the *naya paisa* came into circulation, while the old coins were being withdrawn. Both types of coins— the new and the old— were regarded as legal tender.

One morning, a man called Jamna Singh purchased from a vegetable vendor tomatoes worth two annas and passed on to him a four-anna coin.

The vendor, in return, gave him the required tomatoes and twelve *naya paise*.

Jamna Singh became angry. His objection was that, as a four-anna piece equalled twenty-five *naya paise*, and two annas were only twelve *paise*, he should get one *naya paisa* more.

Jamna Singh's angry tone infuriated the vendor and he harshly answered:— "I have already given you two-annas worth of tomatoes and have returned to you two annas, which is equivalent to twelve *naya paise.*"

Anger led to greater anger. Jamna Singh shouted:— "You dare cheat me! Do you think I am an uneducated man? I shall get one *naya paisa* from you anyhow!"

The vendor was inflamed and shouted back:— "I have given you what is due to you. Get thee gone! I have seen countless people like you. You cannot bully me!"

* Notes of a talk

The dispute came to a head. Jamna Singh took out his *kirpan* (dagger) and mortally wounded the shopkeeper.

The shopkeeper died on the spot. Jamna Singh was handed over to the police and, later, was prosecuted and sentenced to death.

All over one *naya paisa* (which is only a hundredth of a rupee and three thousandth part of a U.S. dollar)!

How true it is that anger is more disastrous than a fire, more disastrous than an earthquake!

In anger, individuals fight each other with dire consequences. In anger, nations fight each other and thousands of young, precious, promising lives are lost.

Gautama Buddha learnt that two kings, with their armies, were ready to fight on the banks of the Rohini. Quickly, he came and stood in their midst. He found that the cause of war was a simple one. Each king claimed for himself the waters of the river Rohini.

He met the kings. He asked them:— "How much is water worth?"

Each king said:— "O Blessed One, water is worth very little!"

"How much," asked the Buddha, "are the kings worth?"

"Great is their worth," was the answer.

"And how much are your queens worth?" asked the Blessed One.

"The queens," answered each king, "are worth much: I love my queen greatly."

"And how much are your soldiers worth?" asked the Buddha.

"Precious to me," answered each king, "is the life of every one of my soldiers. Precious is their life-blood."

Then said the Buddha:— "O ye wise kings, why then are you out to destroy each other and your queens, dear to you, and your soldiers, whose life-blood is precious to you? For the sake of a little water which floweth into the sea! Is not peace better than letting flow a river of blood?"

As the kings listened to the Blessed One, their weapons fell to the ground. They met each other and settled the dispute amicably and thousands of precious lives were saved.

CHAPTER TWO

"You Are A Slave Of My Slave!"

The question was asked of a sage:— "What is it that distinguishes a human being from a brute beast?"

The sage answered:— "Self-control."

The animal cannot control himself: he is a creature of his instincts. Man, if he so desires, can control his cravings and animal appetites, his lust, hatred and greed. Man is meant to be a master of his passions, not to be mastered by them. Alas, many of us are slaves to our desires, cravings, animal appetites.

In the beautiful Sikh Scripture, *Sukhmani*, we have the words:— *kartoota pashu ke, maanush jaat.* So many of us wear human faces, but our lives are no better than those of brute beasts.

A scholar met a beggar, whose clothes were tattered and torn and whose feet were stained with mud: but his brow was broad and radiant, and his eyes were large and luminous.

The scholar was impressed by the beggar's countenance and asked:— "Tell me, who are you?"

"I am a king!" was the answer.

The scholar was amused. "Where is your kingdom, and who are your subjects?" he asked.

"My kingdom is within me," answered the beggar. "And I rule over my feelings and emotions, my senses and the mind."

How many of us can truthfully say that we are masters of our anger and lust and other base emotions? Many of us are no better than animals. True, we wear human faces, but our lives are no better than those of brute beasts. A little thing happens and we feel upset or irritated. A person speaks rudely to us and the colour of our countenance changes. We suffer losses in business, and our sleep is disturbed. Suddenly a dear one is snatched away from us and we lose our faith in God. This is the sad condition of so many of us.

Alexander the Great, as he was about to return from India, remembered that his people had asked him to bring with himself an Indian *yogi*. He set out in quest and found a *yogi* sitting, in a forest, underneath a tree, in silent meditation. Alexander went and sat in front of the *yogi,* in silence.

When the *yogi* opened his eyes, Alexander found that they were lit up with a strange light. He said to the *yogi*:— "Won't you come with me to Greece? I will give you everything you need. A section of the palace will be reserved for you. Servants will wait in attendance and do your bidding."

The *yogi* smiled. "I have no needs," he answered. "I do not need servants to do my bidding. And I have no desire to go to Greece."

The point-blank refusal upset Alexander. He was enraged.

Unsheathing his sword, he said to the *yogi*:— "Do

you know, I can cut you into pieces? I am Alexander, the world conqueror."

The *yogi* smiled again and said quietly:— "You have made two statements. The first is that you can cut me into pieces. No, you cannot cut *me* into pieces. You can only cut the body which is but a garment I have worn. I am immortal, deathless, eternal. And your second statement is that you are a world conqueror. May I tell you, you are only a slave of my slave?"

Intrigued, Alexander said:— "I do not understand."

The *yogi* explained to him:— "Anger is my slave: it is under my control. But you are a slave of anger: how easily you lose your temper! Therefore, are you a slave of my slave!"

An Iranian king said to a scholar:— "Give me a summing up of human life in a few simple words."

The scholar thought for a week, then met the king and said to him:— "Sire, in these few, simple words is given us a summing up of the entire human life:— He was born: he grew in years: he married: he begot children: he died!"

Is this all there is to human life? Those words describe the animal aspect of human existence: but man is more than an animal. It is true, men are born, and so are animals. Men grow in years, so do animals. Men marry. I am not sure if animals also marry, but I know at least of one instance in which an animal couple was brought together in wedlock. I received a wedding card from a wealthy man, inviting his friends to the marriage of his male dog to a female one belonging to another wealthy man. The marriage was to be solemnised in the crystal ball room of a five-star hotel. I cannot say if the couple was faithful to each other, but the marriage did take place.

Man begets children, so do animals. Man dies, and so do animals. Is man only an animal? Is this all there is to human life? Is there not a higher element in human life, which makes the human birth priceless? We must rise from the animal stage of existence to the human. Therefore, we must learn the lesson of self-control.

There was a holy man who arrived in a town. Within a few days, he created an impact upon the people. They spoke highly of him. He is so quiet, they said, so gentle, soft-spoken, sweet, and the very picture of patience. Never have we seen him lose his temper.

A young man heard of the Sadhu and visited him along with his friends. He wanted to find out how patient the Sadhu was.

The young man said to the holy man:— "Sadhuji, I am in need of fire. Will you not give me a little fire?"

"Prabhuji," replied the Sadhu, "I have no fire. I don't need it. I live on food that I get by way of alms."

His friends conversed with the Sadhu concerning spiritual matters. Suddenly, the young man interrupted and said:— "Sadhuji, won't you give me a little fire?"

Once again, the holy man answered sweetly:— "My child, I have already explained to you that there is no fire in my cottage. I do not need it."

This went on. The young man kept on interrupting the Sadhu, again and again, until the holy man lost his temper and flew into a rage. "Dare you interrupt me again!" he shouted. "Get out of this cottage, else I will have you thrown out!"

The young man clapped his hands and said:— "Sadhuji, this is the fire I wanted!"

CHAPTER THREE

The Wild Fire

Anger is a wild fire, a forest fire which spreads from shrub to shrub, from tree to tree, consuming everything that comes its way. In Hindi, we have a couplet which says:— "Anger is the great inflictor of sorrow, the great sinner. First, it sets on fire its own mind, then the fire spreads to others." Anger creates a chain reaction. Someone gets mad at me: I must take it out on someone else, otherwise it will keep on seething within me. That someone else must have it out on yet someone else. And the chain reaction goes on! A boss gets angry at an assistant: the anger is not justified. The poor assistant can't hit back. All that anger keeps on seething within him. As he returns home, he lets it out on his wife. The wife lets it out on the maid–servant. The maid-servant lets it out on one of her children. The child lets it out on a street dog. And the chain reaction goes on. The fire keeps on spreading.

On the surface, we all are good and virtuous. But, within each one of us, there lie hid so many weaknesses and imperfections. The Hindi couplet says further that "under the influence of anger, many of those faults and failings rise to the surface." The worst elements within us are made manifest. Therefore, burn anger before anger burns you.

There is the story of a Russian couple who were deeply in love with each other. Though they had been married for several years, they kept their love fresh.

They made a pact with each other that, every morning, the husband would wake up before the wife and prepare tea. He would bring a cup to his wife and whisper in her ear:— "Honey, here is tea for you!" The wife would wake up with a loving look in her grateful eyes.

You, too, must keep your love fresh. Life, without an element of romance, is dry as the desert-sands. The common complaint of many women is that their husbands take them for granted: they pay them scant attention. This should not be so. Tonight, as you return to your home, go and whisper into the ear of your wife:— "Honey, you mean so much to me!" You will be rewarded with a rich and grateful glow in her eyes. New joy will wake up in her heart. It is such a simple thing. Just try it!

Of a great English poet I read that he never spoke a word of appreciation to his wife. So long as she lived, he criticised her, found fault with many things she did. Suddenly, the wife died. The poet exclaimed:— "Ah, if only you had given me some notice, I would have written poem after poem in your praise, and expressed my heart's gratitude for all that you did for me!"

We recognise the worth of a person only when he is dead. We place wreaths on his dead body and pay glowing tributes to him at memorial meetings. Let us do something for our dear ones, while they are still alive.

Tonight, as you return to your homes, fling a surprise on your wife and let her know how much you love her.

The famous magician, Houdini, kept his love fresh till the very end. He found time, everyday, to write a love-letter to his wife. From 1913 till his death, whether he was in or out of town, he did not let a day pass without writing some words of affection to her.

Keep your love fresh, but do not be attached to

anyone. Attachment is the root of sorrow. No one belongs to you: you belong to the Lord. Therein lies the secret of the art of living. Alone you came into this world: alone, you will leave it. In the mid-period, give as much love as you can to those that cross the pathways of your life. Give love to all, and forgive the wrongs done to you. Give love to all, seeking no revenge for offences and insults.

The great Italian Poet, Tasso, was asked why he did not take revenge upon a man who had hurt him greatly. The Poet answered:— "I do not desire to plunder him: yet there is one thing I would like to take from him."

"His honour, his wealth, his life?", Tasso was asked.

"No," came the gentle reply. "What I desire to take from him, I will try to gain by the exercise of kindness, patience and forbearance. I will try to take away his ill-will." That is the way to burn anger before anger burns us.

The Russian couple kept their love fresh. Every evening, as the husband returned from the office, his wife would wait for him at the gate to welcome him. They would hug each other, enter the house and speak of all that had transpired during the day.

One day, for no fault of the husband, his boss lost his temper and was mad with him for some work which had not been done properly. The husband's feelings were hurt. When he returned home, in the evening, he saw his wife waiting at the gate, but paid her no attention. As he walked into the house, the wife asked:— "Honey, what is the matter? Has something gone wrong?" Tell me, if only to take the burden off your mind!"

The irate husband blurted out:— "Why must you keep on chattering all the time? Why don't you shut up? I do not want to hear your silly voice anymore."

The wife was stunned. The lotus of her heart

drooped and she promised never to speak to her husband again:— "He does not want to hear my silly voice! I shall not let him hear it."

This went on for forty years. The husband, of course, repented. Repeatedly, he begged forgiveness. But the wound created, in the heart of the wife, by those sharp, angry words was too deep. She could never make up her mind to speak to her husband. He was now on his death-bed. He pleaded with her:— "Pray, speak just one word of forgiveness to me, so that I may die in peace." She felt helpless. Words just would not come out of her lips.

CHAPTER FOUR

When To Be Angry

The very first lesson that was taught to every student in ancient India was:— "*Satyam vada, krodham maakuru!*" "Always speak the truth and never yield to anger!" This is the teaching that needs to be passed on to every student:— "Always speak the truth; and howsoever strong the provocation, never yield to anger." Burn anger before anger burns your happiness and peace.

If anger is such an evil thing, why did God create it? Anger was created so that we could be angry at our own selves— for we turn our faces again and again from the Light and become victims to lust, hatred, greed. Anger is a weapon which has been given to us for self-improvement. Instead, we direct our anger at others and degrade ourselves.

A woman complained to Sadhu Vaswani:— "I have prayed to God, again and again, to grant me the gift of the new life, but He does not listen."

Sadhu Vaswani said:— "Why don't you use the stick?"

The woman was shocked. "How can I strike God with a stick?" she asked.

Sadhu Vaswani said:— "Strike yourself!"

Anger is a two-edged sword. There is a type of anger which drains energy and produces tension. There is another type of anger that is a positive and a creative life-force.

There is a type of anger which is known as righteous anger. When it is my duty to be angry, and I become angry—that is righteous anger. A parent has sometimes to be angry with a child for the good of the child. A teacher has sometimes to be angry with a student for the good of the student. An employer has sometimes to be angry with an employee for the good of the organisation.

Jesus got angry with the temple priests when he found them selling birds in the temple. In anger, Jesus said:— "What have you done? You have converted my Father's House into a business centre!" This is an example of righteous anger.

If you find a man molesting a woman or ill-treating an animal on the roadside, you have every right to be angry. Anger becomes righteous when you get angry to defend the rights of another, without any selfish motive.

CHAPTER FIVE

Why Must I Not Be Angry?

When a person gets angry, he activates certain glands in the body. This leads to an outpouring of adrenaline and other stress harmones, with noticeable physical consequences. The face reddens, blood pressure increases, the voice rises to a higher pitch, breathing becomes faster and deeper, the heart-beats become harder, the muscles of the arms and legs tighten. The body moves into an excited state.

If a man is given to anger, all these processes are repeated, again and again, and the man is surely heading towards serious health problems. The cumulative effect of the hormones released during anger episodes can add to the risk of coronary and other life-threatening diseases, including strokes, ulcers, high blood pressure. It is, therefore, in your own interest that you learn to control—or, in any case, reduce—your anger.

Recent researches have proved that people who are easily prone to anger get heart attacks more easily than those that are not so easily prone to anger. Burn anger, before anger burns you!

It has also been proved that when a person is calm, peaceful, happy, the digestive processes work normally. When man comes under the influence of anger, the digestive processes are paralysed. Therefore, doctors recommend that you should be cheerful and in good humour when you eat. If you don't feel cheerful, it is better that you lay off from your eating.

Stomach ulcers are caused by anger. They recur even after operations, if the resentment continues.

Anger affects the entire body, for anger is poison. I read concerning a mother who was given to frequent bouts of anger. Her infant received milk from her while she was in angry moods. Soon the baby died. Anger throws poison into the blood stream.

CHAPTER SIX

Three Ways Of Handling Anger

There are three ways of handling anger. There is, firstly, the way of expression. Psychiatrists tell us that it is good to express anger. Expression gives you relief, for you get some satisfaction at having given a piece of your mind to the other person. This relief, however, is temporary. Resentments build up again, and you are ready for another spill out. Gradually, anger becomes a habit: a time comes when you become a slave to anger. You are controlled by anger: and anger is a terrible master. I read concerning a mother. In a mood of anger, she threw her own child into the fire!

The second is the way of suppression. It is not the right way. Suppression drives anger into the subconscious: there it works its subconscious havoc.

I read of a girl whose right arm was paralysed. She could not lift it up . On investigation, it was found that the girl, when angry, had a strong desire to strike her mother. She suppressed the desire and it entered the subconscious and paralysed the arm. When the fact was brought to her notice, she gave up her resentments and the arm was restored to normal health.

Expression is not the right way. Expression is very much like a cyst. You have it operated upon and get relief for some time. But the cyst gets filled up again, and you are in for another operation.

Suppression is not the right way. Through suppression, we push our resentments into the subconscious where they may develop into a complex and affect our entire behaviour and attitude towards life.

The right way is the way of forgiveness, of patience and forbearance. Forgive, and be free! Every night, before you retire, actually go over the happenings of the day. Has someone cheated you? Has someone offended you? Has someone hurt you or ill-treated you? Call out that person's name and say, "Mr. X, I forgive you!" "Mrs. Y, I forgive you!" "Miss Z, I forgive you!" You will have a peaceful sleep and beautiful dreams. The right way to overcome anger is the way of forgiveness.

In one of his sermons, which he preached in the tropical forests of Africa, Dr. Albert Schweitzer said to the black people:— You get up in the morning and a wicked man comes and abuses you and covers you with insults. You do not get angry: you merely smile at him and in the heart within pray for him. Later in the day, your neighbour's goat eats up a whole bunch of bananas you had brought from the garden for dinner. You complain to the neighbour and ask for compensation, but he denies that it was his goat. Take it easy and go in peace. Be consoled with the thought that God makes many more bunches of bananas to grow in your plantation. A little later, you meet the man to whom you had given ten bunches of bananas for selling them in the market and he gives you money for nine and insists that you gave him nine bunches and not ten. You feel tempted to call him a liar. But you think of all the lies for which God has pardoned you. And you let the man go and be at peace. You are ready to light the fire and cook your noon meal and you find that someone has stolen the firewood you had collected. Your temperature rises and you feel the rage within you. But your heart compels you to pardon the culprit and abandon the desire to make the round of the huts in the vicinity to identify the thief. Today, when evening comes, you can go to bed in peace and be happy because you were able to pardon the numerous hurts you received during the day.

Yes— the right way to burn anger is to breathe out peace to all. We have that beautiful Vedic hymn which says:—

> *To the heavens be peace:*
> *To the sky and the earth,*
> *To the waters be peace!*
> *To plants and all trees,*
> *To the gods be peace,*
> *To Brahma be peace,*
> *To all men be peace,*
> *Again and again—*
> *Peace also to me!*

I recall an incident in the life of the great Prussian king— Frederick the Second. One day, he found one of his servants taking a little snuff from his silver snuff-box.

"Do you like this snuff–box?" asked the king in utter simplicity.

The boy servant, realising that he was caught in the act of stealing, felt embarrassed and hung his head low in shame. He did not answer.

Once again, the king repeated the question:— "Do you like the snuff–box?"

The boy looked up and said:— "Yes sire, it is

indeed a beautiful snuff–box!"

"Then," said the king, "take it. For it is too small for the two of us!"

Of Hasan it is said, that one day, one of his slaves accidentally dropped a cup of hot soup on Hasan's clothes and hands.

Frightened, the slave immediately quoted a verse from the Qur'an:— "Paradise belongs to those who control their anger."

Hasan immediately replied:— "I am not angry!"

The slave continued:— "Paradise belongs to those who forgive the offender!"

Hasan said:— "I forgive you!"

The slave quoted the last words of the verse:— "Above all, Paradise belongs to those who return good for evil!"

"I release you and give you freedom," said Hasan to the slave and also gave him ten gold coins.

Forgiveness is the right way to deal with anger. To burn anger, we must develop the quality of forgiveness.

There was a monk who had a bad temper. He lived in an *ashram* but found it difficult to get along with the *ashramites.* He decided to leave the *ashram* and live a life of a *tapasvin* in the forest. He thought he could conquer anger, if only he lived a secluded life. In the beginning he found peace and tranquillity within him. He was extremely happy.

One day, he went to the river to fill a jug of water. As he kept the jug on the ground, it toppled over. He picked it up and filled it again. Again, the jug toppled down. He repeated the process for a number of times, until finally he lost his temper and smashed the jug into pieces.

Then it was that he realised his mistake. "I left the *ashram*", he confessed, " only to contol my anger, but anger has followed me even here into the forest."

It is not individuals or situations that cause anger. It is one's own reaction or response to individuals and situations that determines whether we will be angry or otherwise.

CHAPTER SEVEN

12 Practical Suggestions

PRACTICAL SUGGESTION NO. 1

The best and the surest way of controlling anger is the way of self-realisation.

Once you realise what you are, you will never be angry. It is only because we identify ourselves with the bodies that we wear, that we succumb to anger. It is the sense of separateness that is the cause of anger. Once you realise that you are the universal self— the self that is in you, in me, in everyone of us— how can you be angry? Sometimes, your hand scratches your arm and blood oozes out. The arm does not retaliate. The arm knows that both the arm and the hand belong to one body. Once we realise that we all are parts of the One Whole, we will never get angry. If I behold myself in you, how can I be angry with you? The one solution to all our problems is self-realisation.

Self-realisation cannot be achieved overnight. We have to live a life of *sadhana* (discipline). To achieve self-realisation, the practice of silence is very essential. You must keep your daily appointment with God. Everyday, preferably at the same time and at the same place, sit in silence and put to yourself the question again and again:— "What am I?"

Man, today, knows so much concerning the universe in which he lives. Man has stationed satellites in space. Man's rockets go flying past the distant planets. But how little does man know about himself?

Sitting in silence, put to yourself the simple question:— "What am I?" Gradually, out of the depths within you, will come an answer. You will realise that you are not this body that you wear. You are not the mind. The body is only an instrument, a garment which you have worn, and the mind is an instrument you have brought with yourself to carry out your work on the physical plane. You are not the body: you are not the mind: you are not the intellect. You are THAT! *Tat Twam Asi!* That art Thou! Self-realisation and anger cannot live together even as light and darkness cannot dwell together.

PRACTICAL SUGGESTION NO. 2

Develop the will-to-control anger. Realise the uselessness of anger.

When we get angry, we may not harm the person with whom we are angry, but we are definitely harming ourselves. The Gita says:— "Man is his own friend and man is his own foe." When I succumb to anger, I become my own enemy. I may not be hurting the other person, but surely I hurt myself. I throw poison into the blood stream.

There was a man who was given to frequent bursts of anger. Over every trifle, he would lose his temper. After some time, they found that a change had come over him. He had become calm and gentle. Nothing could excite him. You could never make him angry. Asked the reason for the tremendous change, he said:— "Every morning as I wake up, I say to myself:— 'This new day comes to me out of the spotless Hands of the Lord. I have before me the choice— either to be angry or not to be angry.' The choice I make is never to be angry. Then, throughout the day, I keep on reminding myself that I have made the choice and I must be true to it. Come what may, I must not lose my temper at least for this one day. People may not treat me properly, things may not turn out the way I want them to, but this one day I must never be angry. I may be angry tomorrow, surely not today."

Develop the will-not-to-be-angry. Some of you may work on this plan. Tomorrow morning, as you wake up, say to yourself:— There is a choice before you— either to be angry or not to be angry. Make your choice. Once you have made it, you must stick to it.

PRACTICAL SUGGESTION NO. 3

Rejoice in whatever the Will of God brings to you.

Have you ever asked yourselves:— What is the root–cause of anger? The root–cause of anger is self-will. I want things to happen in a particular way, they have happened in a different way. I become angry. When our desires are crossed, we lose our temper. At the root of all anger is self-will. I wanted a particular dish for my dinner: I find that something different has been made. I lose my temper. If only I can understand that everything happens according to the Will of God, and in the Will of God is man's highest good, I will not get angry. I will learn to accept everything. This happens through practice of daily silence. Everyday, sit in silence, and explain to yourself that not a leaf stirs, except it be the Will of God and in the Will of God is our real good, though appearances may be to the contrary. Through practice, I will arrive at a stage of stability where nothing will upset me and make me angry.

There was a scientist who worked, at the turn of the century, on barometric pressures. Everyday, he would watch the barometer several times and note down readings. For twenty long years, he did his work. He decided to make a study of all those readings and formulate a theory.

His maid-servant asked for a holiday and left a substitute. In the evening, as the scientist went out for his usual walk, he noted down the reading. On his return, he took the reading but could not note it down, as he found his papers missing. He asked the new maid-servant where the papers were.

"Sir," she answered, "I was cleaning your table, when I noticed all those dirty, stained sheets of paper. I burnt them in the fire and have kept new, clean sheets in their place."

The Professor's labour of twenty long years was lost in a moment. But he did not utter one angry word. He only said:— "Lord, Thy Will be done!"

Later, the Professor learnt that there was a meaning of mercy in all that had happened. Some other scientist, in a distant country, had worked on the same problem and already published a book. Had the sheets not been burnt, he would have been put to a lot of unnecessary trouble in compiling the figures, arranging them, working out a theory and publishing a book which would have served no purpose, as a similiar one was already in the market.

The plan of God may or may not be revealed to us. But we must never forget that there is always some hidden good in everything that happens. Therefore, let us greet every incident and accident of life with the words:— "I accept!" It will, then, not be difficult for us to control our anger.

PRACTICAL SUGGESTION NO. 4

If you wish to control your anger, you must seek the help of the Super-Power, whom for want of a better word, we call God.

There was a time when I was given to frequent spells of anger. Little things would trigger me off. I tried my best to control my temper, but would succeed only for two or three days. Suddenly, my pent-up emotions would burst and I would break down over a matter of no significance. I would repent: I would shed tears. This went on, until I placed my difficulty before my beloved Master, Sadhu Vaswani. He said to me:— "Why don't you give up your proud conviction that, unaided, you can undo your *karma?*. Go to God! Seek His help. And the impossible can become possible!" I tried this, and it worked!

God is both our Father and Mother. In such situations, it is helpful to appeal to the Mother-aspect of God and say to Her:— "Ma! I come to Thee in this state of utter helplessness. I have tried a hundred times and failed every time. I cannot do it on my own. It is only when Thy Wisdom and Thy Strength flow into me that I will be able to stand up and face every situation and come out victorious! But the victory is not mine: the victory is all Thine! *Jai Jai Jai Jagadambha! Jai Jai Jai Jagadambha!*"

Try this experiment: it will work! Keep on repeating this prayer in the heart within, as many times as you can:— and you will, by God's grace, be blessed with results on the very first day.

PRACTICAL SUGGESTION NO. 5

Avoid the occasion.

Whenever you find you are in the presence of a situation which may cause you to be angry, turn away from it.

They brought to Julius Caeser, the dictator of Rome, papers in which one of his enemies had disparaged him.

"If I read those papers," Julius Caeser said, "I will unnecessarily become angry. I won't be harming that man, but will surely harm myself!" Instead, he ordered that the papers be burnt. Avoid occasions!

PRACTICAL SUGGESTION NO. 6

Avoid haste.

Haste is the mother of anger, as hatred is its father. Never be in a hurry to do anything. Avoid overwork. Go about your work quietly, lovingly, gently. The very thought of overwork sometimes leads to anger.

There is a man who, as he wakes up in the morning, prepares a long list of the many things he has to attend to during the day. The list is a long one and so, naturally, he feels overworked. Not that all those items are attended to during the day: several are carried forward to the list he prepares on the following day. All the time he lives in the thought that he has a lot of work to do. This makes him lose his patience, time and again.

One day, a visitor entered his office and was met with an angry look. Quietly, he walked out and, later, mentioned to a friend:— "I just wanted to pass on to him a cheque for Rs. 50,000/- for the good work his organisation is doing!" The overworked man did not realise what he had lost!

On the other hand, there is the instance of a laboratory technician, who had to analyse 175 samples on a particular day. The boss sympathised with him, saying:— "You have to handle 175 samples today. You must be feeling overworked!"

Quietly answered the technician:— "Sir, I can handle only one sample at a time. I concentrate on the sample before me. I never feel overworked!"

PRACTICAL SUGGESTION NO. 7

Whenever you feel anger approaching, keep your mouth shut, your lips sealed.

A woman came to a holy man and complained:—
"Whenever there is an argument, my husband beats
me."

The holy man asked for a bottle of water. "I will
bless it and give it to you," he said.

"When do I give this water to my husband to
drink?" the woman asked.

"The water is not for your husband," exclaimed
the holy man. "Whenever you find that an argument
has started, take a sip of water from this bottle and
hold it in your mouth! In doing so, you will not be
able to answer back and the question of beating will
not arise!"

Many of our problems would be solved if only
we kept our mouths shut. We try to explain things
and, in the process, complicate them. We have the
words in an ancient book:— "All your answers are
great and excellent, and which a man can hardly
understand." Truth has its own way of being out at
the right time.

Keep the mouth shut. Therefore, begin by
observing *mauna* (silence) for at least two hours
everyday. Once you acquire the taste of silence, you
will not wish to speak, unless there is a great need to
do so. Keep the mouth shut—and when you open it,
speak softly, lovingly, gently.

PRACTICAL SUGGESTION NO. 8

If you are unable to keep your mouth shut, hum to yourself a simple tune.

A simple tune such as:—
Deena-bandhu, Deenaa-naath,
Meri dori Tere haath!
or
Tum bin meri kaun khabar lay,
Govardhana Girdhaari?

Merely humming a tune will take away the anger out of you. If you like, you may utter the sacred syllable, "*Om! Om! Om!*" Repetition of the sacred word will fill you with peace and joy. Or you may take a few deep breaths evenly and deeply: this will help you to relax and remain calm.

PRACTICAL SUGGESTION NO. 9

When angry, drink a glass or two of cold water. Or go out and take a brisk walk, or run, or jog.

The idea is to burn up the emotional energy that has awakened. When the energy is burnt out, anger will automatically subside.

PRACTICAL SUGGESTION NO. 10

Count upto ten. Or if you find the emotion of anger is strong, count upto a hundred.

Julius Caeser, when angry, would repeat the letters of the Roman alphabet, before uttering a word.

PRACTICAL SUGGESTION NO. 11

Develop a sense of humour.

Humour saves us from many a difficult situation.

A couple was married for ten long years. One day, the husband got angry and complained to a friend:— "When we were married, my wife used to bring me my slippers and my dog barked. Now the process has reversed. The dog brings me the slippers, and my wife barks."

The wife heard those words, but did not get angry. She had a sense of humour. Immediately, she said to her husband:—"Darling, of what are you complaining? You continue to get the same service!"

PRACTICAL SUGGESTION NO. 12

Cultivate an understanding heart.

Put yourself in the other person's place before you decide to get angry with him. Try to understand his point of view. Very often, we jump to conclusions which, in most cases, are wrong. King Solomon prayed:— "God, grant me an understanding heart!"

The man with an understanding heart, will not be easily angered. Concerning such a one the Lord says in the Bhagavad Gita:—

> *In sorrow not dejected,*
> *In joy not overjoyed!*
> *Outside the influence of passion,*
> *Of fear and anger,*
> *Ever calm in sorrow and joy—*
> *Such a one is wise, indeed!*

The Miracle
Of
Understanding

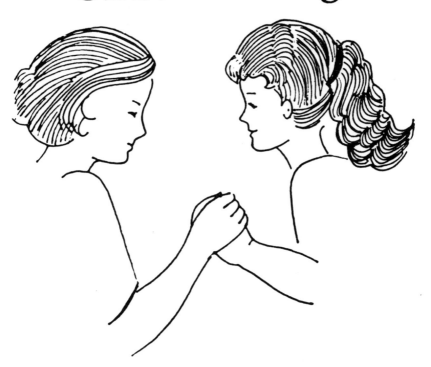

The greatest famine in the world is the famine of understanding. No two people seem to understand each other.

Today, people speak of emotional incompatibility. It is a myth invented by jurists and lawyers to be able to argue in favour of divorce.

There are no emotional incompatibilities. There are only misunderstandings and mistakes which can be corrected where there is the will to do so.

CHAPTER ONE

The Great Famine*

There was a woman. One day, as she walked, she was surprised to find a man hoeing his garden, while sitting on a chair. "What laziness!" the woman exclaimed. After a while, as she carefully looked at the chair, she found lying by its side a pair of crutches. She realised that the man who was hoeing the garden, was a cripple. Criticism immediately changed into admiration, and she praised the man who, despite his handicap, was so eager to work.

The woman learnt the lesson of her life, never to make snap judgments, never to jump to conclusions without first understanding the situation in which the other person was placed. It is understanding that is needed.

There was another woman. She received her daily supply of vegetables from a hawker, who came to her house, at the right time, everyday. One day, as she was entertaining guests, she waited for the hawker to arrive, but he failed to come. The woman felt let down. She was naturally upset. The next day, when the hawker came at the right time, she spoke harshly to him:— "You are the most unreliable person I have ever seen: you let me down yesterday! When I needed vegetables, you did not turn up!"

After her tirade was over, the hawker gently said to her:—"I am so sorry for having caused you inconvenience. Yesterday, suddenly, my mother

* Notes of a talk

expired, and I had to carry the body to the cremation ground."

The woman felt ashamed of having spoken harshly and promised never to do so, until she had first understood the situation in which the other person was placed. It is understanding that we need.

There was a spiritual aspirant, a devotee of the Lord. One day, as he sat in his house, an able-bodied man came and asked for food. The devotee looked at the man and said to him:— "Aren't you ashamed of begging? You are able-bodied. Why don't you work and earn your livelihood?" The man did not argue. He only said to the devotee:— "Thank you! And may God bless you!"

That night, the devotee had a dream in which he found his spiritual Master asking him to eat a dead body that lay on the floor. The devotee did not wish to disobey the Master. "But how can I eat a dead body?" he asked. And the Master said to him:— "You did eat a dead body this morning! Do you know that the man you criticised is a holy man who lives, in the forest, a life of meditation and prayer? He eats only fruits and roots. Every morning, he comes to the river to fill his jug of water. This morning, as he came to the river, he found a man drowning in the waters. Immediately, he plunged into the river and saved the life of the drowning man. He gave him artificial respiration: and when he came back to consciousness, asked him to wait until he brought for him some little food from the town."

How many dead bodies will we continue to eat, day after day?

Is it not true that the one urgent and piteous need of the world, today, is understanding? Understanding among individuals and families, among neighbours and groups, among the nations of the earth. We cannot have international understanding until, first, the hearts of the people become understanding hearts, even as we cannot have international peace until, first, there is peace in the hearts of men. I recall the words of Sadhu Vaswani:— "How can you have peace on earth when the hearts of men are a volcano?"

The greatest famine in the world, today, is the famine of understanding. No two people seem to be able to understand one another. That is why we hear those words being uttered again and again:— "Why don't you understand me?" The age we live in is an age in which misunderstandings abound— misunderstandings in our homes, in our clubs, in our schools, colleges, universities, in our temples and churches. I recall the words of the great Parsi Prophet, Zoroaster:— "Know well, that a hundred temples of wood and stone have not the value of one single understanding heart!" Understanding hearts are needed.

King Solomon prayed:— "Lord! Thou hast granted me so many things. Grant me one thing more. Grant me an understanding heart." Understanding hearts are needed.

Today, brain power has been developed, technological progress has been made, science is marching on. But the problems that are before civilisation today, will not be solved by the developed brain alone. Understanding, awakened, illumined hearts are needed.

Science has given us many good things— gadgets, comforts, conveniences. But science has done nothing to give us the spirit of understanding. I recall an amusing incident in the life of the great Russian leader, Maxim Gorky. One day, he addressed a large rally of peasants. He spoke to them on the "Benefits of Science". He said:— "Science has taught man how to fly in the air like a bird. And science has taught man how to dive into the depths of an ocean like a fish!" Then it is that a simple, illiterate, uneducated peasant gets up and says:— "Sir! what you say is only too true. Science has taught man how to fly in the air like a bird and science has taught man how to dive into the depths of an ocean like a fish, but science has not taught man how to live on earth as a man, in goodwill, amity and peace with his fellow-men!"

Science has given us so many wonderful things: DDT for killing insects, 2–4–D for killing weeds, formula 1080 for killing rats. And science has also given us that fatal equation, $E = mc^2$, which is capable of wiping out populations. When scientists learnt how to split the atom and release the tremendous power that lies locked up within its nucleus, the very first use they made of the discovery was to rain death and destruction on Nagasaki and Hiroshima. The problem of science lies in its misuse. Because we have not grown in the spirit of understanding, science has become more of a curse than a blessing.

CHAPTER TWO

Dialogues Of The Deaf

A young man came to his father, who was a *rishi*, a sage. The young man said:— "Father, I seek knowledge!"

The father said to him:— "My child, get thee understanding!"

The son said again:— "Father, I seek power!"

Once again, the father said to him:— "My child, get thee understanding!"

Knowledge is good and power is good. But without the spirit of understanding, both knowledge and power are being perverted into instruments of social chaos and destruction. It is the spirit of understanding that is needed. If we would grow in the spirit of understanding, we need to develop the will-to-understand. This is very important. The intense desire to understand must be there in our hearts.

Two years ago, I was in Switzerland. There I met a wonderful man. Our difficulty was how to communicate with each other. I do not know French, and he knew only a few words of the English language. Even so, we managed to get through to one another, because there was the ardent desire to do so. It is this desire that is very necessary.

This is the very first condition of developing an understanding heart: we must have the will-to-understand. On the face of it, this statement might appear quite commonplace. But let me tell you, the will-to-understand, the intense desire-to-understand is far more rare than we think. Listen to the conversations of the world— the conversations between nations and individuals. I have listened to conversations between couples. I often call them the "dialogues of the deaf". Each one is anxious to set forth his own ideas, in order to justify himself, to defend his position, to make himself appear greater than he truly is, and to accuse others. There is scarcely a desire to understand the other person.

Think of the little things over which we quarrel. A wife said that she could not sleep until she had read something for a while. The husband said he could not sleep if the light was on. The wife switched on the light and the husband switched it off. This led to a quarrel, and the quarrel went on, until both of them felt tired and went off to sleep, with evil thoughts in their minds, ready to restart the war at the earliest opportunity, the next morning. The spirit of understanding was lacking.

The wife could have got a bedside table lamp,

which would not disturb the husband in his sleep. But there is the ego-problem: and the ego is something that will never give up.

A man was eating his breakfast when his wife emerged out of the bathroom. She looked annoyed. When she went in, she had been in a cheerful mood. The husband asked her what was wrong and she answered:— "No, nothing is wrong!"

The husband insisted:— "Apparently, there is something that is wrong. Tell me!"

She said:— "Okay, I will tell you. How many times have I not told you that I cannot stand it, if you squeeze the middle of the toothpaste tube? Why don't you squeeze it at the bottom?"

The husband said:— "What does it matter, if I squeeze it at the middle?"

And so the quarrel ensued and the quarrel went on and on. The spirit of understanding is lacking. Every problem has a solution. The wife could have got a separate toothpaste tube for herself. But there is the ego-problem. And the ego is something that will never give up.

A couple came from New York and met me. The wife complained that her husband was so busy with his work that he could not find any time for her. She felt neglected, ignored. The husband did not defend his position. He said :— "What she says is perfectly true. From now on, I promise to take her out every Wednesday evening, to the movies or wherever she chooses." That was a step in the right direction. Every Wednesday evening, he did take her out, but there was no attempt made by him to understand her. What his wife needed was understanding.

We may go out together every evening, we may live together for years, but if the spirit of understanding is lacking, we cannot draw close to each other. This is the situation in so many outstanding, cultured, intelligent families, today. People of the very highest order, successful businessmen, big industrialists, learned professors— in their families the spirit of understanding is lacking. It is understanding that will draw them closer and knit them into a unity which not all the changing vicissitudes of life may break.

Today, we hear so much of emotional incompatibility. I do not believe in it. I regard it as a myth invented by jurists and lawyers so that they can argue in favour of divorce. There are no emotional incompatibilities. There are only misunderstandings and mistakes which can be corrected, where there is the will to do so.

Women have come and said to me:— "In the days of courtship, we seemed to understand each other. Our husbands said, we are made for each other. What has happened to us now? And why?" The reason is a simple one. In the days of courtship, they talked to each other, they opened up to one another. They found great pleasure in understanding and in being understood.

CHAPTER THREE

Seven Practical Suggestions

I would now wish to pass on to you some practical suggestions on how to grow in the spirit of understanding. Understanding leads to harmony and harmony is the essence of music. Even as the musical scale has seven notes, even so, the musical scale of understanding has seven notes. I would wish to pass on to you seven practical suggestions. It is not necessary that all the seven be put into practice simultaneously. It is enough if we choose but one of them and try to live up to it in deeds of daily living. We will be richly rewarded.

PRACTICAL SUGGESTION NO. 1

Learn to be a good listener.

If you wish to grow in the spirit of understanding, you must let the other person talk and prove his point to his satisfaction. Do not interrupt him, while he is talking. You know how exasperated you become when someone interrupts you, while you are trying to prove a point. At committee meetings, I have heard those words uttered quite often:— "But let me finish!"

Listen more, talk less. You are made to listen. That is why you have been given only one mouth and two ears. If we were meant to talk more and listen less, we would have been given only one ear, right in front, and two mouths on the two sides. How funny we would look! And, mind you, there is no door with which to close the ears: they are always open. Before a word can be spoken, it has to cross two fences— two rows of teeth and two lips. Therefore, think twice before you talk. Never forget that of the unspoken word, you are a master, of the spoken word, you are a slave. Words, once spoken, cannot be got back.

I am reminded of an amusing little incident. A villager came to a town, to visit some of his relatives. In villages, till today, they cleanse their teeth with wooden sticks. When he got up in the morning, the villager asked for one. They told him that in the cities they had only toothpaste tubes. The villager had never handled a toothpaste tube. As he squeezed it, out flowed a foot-long strip of toothpaste. He was taken aback. "Is there a way of sending the toothpaste back into the tube?" he asked. They said to him:— "No way! Once the paste has come out, it cannot be sent in!" Likewise, words which have been spoken cannot be sent in.

Be a good listener. Therefore, listen not only with the ears, but also with the heart. Better than talking is listening. And better than listening is to enter the silence within.

The great woman-saint of South India, Avvaiyar, prayed:— "O God, what is happening to me? I keep on talking and talking, as though there were mouths all over my body! When shall I cease from doing this? When shall I enter into the silence within?"

PRACTICAL SUGGESTION NO. 2

Do not belittle the other person. Do not make him feel small. Do not criticise him or find fault with him.

No one likes to be criticised. Look for good qualities in others and appreciate them. When you appreciate others, you draw out the best that is in them. Appreciate your friends, your spouse, your children. Never scold children. When you scold them, you stifle the life–force that is within them.

I asked a little boy:— "My child, what is your name?"

He answered:— "At school, they call me Ramesh. At home, I am called Ramesh-don't."

I could not understand. And he explained :— "At school they call me Ramesh. But whenever I am at home, they always tell me, Ramesh don't behave like this, Ramesh don't speak like this, Ramesh don't sit like this, Ramesh don't talk like this!"

Appreciate your children. Appreciate your spouse. Women have complained to me :— "There was a time when our husbands gave us many pledges, but all that has become part of history. Today, they pay no attention to us. They take us for granted."

Tonight, as you return to your homes, go and tell your spouse:— "Honey, where would I have been without you?" Those few, simple words can enact a miracle. When I was in Hong Kong, at one of the lectures, a leading man of Hong Kong presided. At the meeting, I offered this suggestion. And the man, who presided over the meeting, met me the next day. He said:— "Truly, the words you passed on to us yesterday, have enacted a miracle. When I returned home last night, I told my wife, 'Honey, where would I have been without you?' At first, my wife could not understand. Her face was blank. Then, gradually, as the meaning of those words became clear, her face brightened and her eyes glowed with a strange light. Since then, the entire atmosphere of the house has changed!"

PRACTICAL SUGGESTION NO. 3

When you find you cannot get along well with others, do not blame them. Find the fault in yourself.

It is easy to blame others, but it does not help. When you find that things are not going well, ask yourself:— What have I done? Where have I gone wrong? You will find that your relationship with others will immediately improve.

PRACTICAL SUGGESTION NO. 4

There can be no true understanding without the spirit of humility.

It is only when you grow humble that you can truly understand. The word, "understand", says:— "stand under". No one is prepared, today, to stand under anyone. Everybody wants to stand over everybody. That is the main cause of misunderstandings. That is why the man of humility will never misunderstand others. He will never give himself airs. He will never show that he is superior to others.

The conversation of so many of us is full of the pronoun, "I". I did this, I did that. I gave this, I gave that. I achieved this, I achieved that. The man of humility will rarely use the pronoun "I". His conversation is full of the pronouns, "we" and "you".

Mary Anderson, the contralto, often used "we" and "one" instead of the personal "I". When they asked her what was the reason, she answered:— "One realises, the longer one lives, that there is no particular thing one can do alone. With the execution of the work we do, there are many people involved... so the "I" in it is very small, after all."

A mother of twins related a conversation she heard between the children.

One twin said to another:— "Remember, *I* am the I, you are only you!"

The other immediately said:— "*I* am the I, you are only you!"

Louder, said the first one:— "Did *I* not tell you, *I* am the I, and you are only you?"

So it went on, until they got so excited that they began to fight each other.

How often do we not, in our daily life, behave like the twins? It is I, I, I, all the time. The ego keeps on playing its game, singing its tune. The ego is the cause of misunderstandings–and so much of our suffering.

Oscar Hammerstein, the famous actor and producer, had an advertisement inserted in the Christmas issue of *Variety*, where actors and producers display their successes. In his advertisement, Oscar Hammerstein did not refer to his achievements. He merely listed five of his failures, stating at the bottom in big, bold letters:— "I did it before, and I can do it again."

All the great ones of humanity have been men and women of humility. One day, they asked St. Francis of Assisi:— "Tell us, why is it that the whole world is running after you. You are not handsome. You are not learned. You are not wealthy. You do not hold a high position."

The saint, in utter humility, answered:— "There is nothing in me. It is all due to the grace of God."

And they asked him:— "Why is it that of all persons God chose you, on whom to pour His grace?"

The saint answered:— "God set out in quest of the most wretched man on earth on whom to pour His grace so that He could demonstrate what His grace could do. He could not find a man more wretched than I!"

PRACTICAL SUGGESTION NO. 5

The man of understanding argues little.

How true it is that no one ever wins an argument. When you think you have won an argument, sooner or later, you will discover that you have not convinced the other person. You have only worn him out. In the process, you may have lost a friend.

For forty years, a man had refused to have anything to do with his only brother. Just because the other brother would rather win an argument than have his brother's respect and love.

PRACTICAL SUGGESTION NO. 6

The man of understanding knows what it is to agree, despite differences. Even when he does not agree, he respects the other person. He never indulges in backbiting. He does not compare himself or his partner with

**others. He forgets his ego. He practises what
he preaches.**

It is very easy to give advice to others. It is very easy to tell your partner to do this or that. But if you do not practise what you preach, no one will pay attention.

There is a touching incident in the life of Mahatma Gandhi. One day, a mother came to him, saying:— "My child suffers from a kidney disease. The doctors have asked him to refrain from eating salt, but he does not listen. He is devoted to you and will gladly do your bidding."

Mahatma Gandhi said to her :— "Bring your son to me after a week!"

After seven days, the mother and son met Mahatma Gandhi, who requested the little boy not to take salt. The boy immediately agreed.

The mother was puzzled. She asked the Mahatma, why he did not give the advice a week earlier?

Mahatmaji said to her:— "When you came to me last week, I used to take salt with my food. I said to myself that before I could advise another to refrain from eating salt, I must do it myself. This whole week I have refrained from eating salt and so feel qualified to give the advice."

PRACTICAL SUGGESTION NO. 7

**The man of understanding is always on the
lookout for opportunities to be of service to
others.**

In big cities like Bombay, Madras, Calcutta, London, New York, wherever I have gone, I have found that the people are indifferent to the needs of others. They are indifferent to the point of callousness. May I tell you what is the opposite of love? The opposite of love is not hatred, but apathy, indifference to the needs of those around you. If you wish to grow in the spirit of understanding, you must grow in the spirit of service. You must look out for opportunities to be of service to others.

A boy asked his mother:— "Ma! why are we here?"

She answered:— "We are here to help others."

The boy was not satisfied. He asked:— "What are the others here for?"

Those of us, who would wish to grow in the spirit of understanding, do not have to ask, what are the others here for? We have only to understand that we are here to help others.

I read concerning a young man. He travelled by a railway train. In his compartment was an old man who appeared nervous and fidgety. The young man went and sat by his side and asked if he could do anything to help. The old man explained to him that, early in the morning, he received a telegram informing him that his only son had been taken seriously ill and had been shifted to a hospital, situated in a town at which the train would arrive late in the night. "My anxiety," he said, "is how to find the Hospital at that late hour of the night." The young man assured him that he should not be worried on that account. "I have lived for some days in the town," he said to the old man, "and know exactly where the Hospital is situated. I will get down at the station with you, take you to the Hospital, then return to the station and catch the next train for my destination!"

There was a man who had the true spirit of understanding.

* * *

A couple wanted to adopt a child. They visited an orphanage. A boy particularly interested them. They said to him:— "If you stay with us, we will get you picture-books and games and sweets and toys and a

T.V." The boy did not seem interested.

So they asked him:— "What is it that you need?"

He answered:— " I do not need toys and sweets and games and picture-books. Nor a T. V. All I need is someone who will understand me!"

Is that not the hunger of every human heart? Everyone wants someone to understand him or her. But here lies the great paradox of understanding. You will not receive understanding until first you forget yourself and give understanding to others. The understanding that goes out of you will come back to you. For, understanding moves in a circle.

The world, today, is passing through a period of crisis. Unrest in all the countries of the world is deepening. The nations are moving in a jungle of darkness. Passion for power, lust for fame, greed of gold grow from more to more. Humanity, today, stands on the brink of a precipice. Humanity is on the point of committing suicide. Humanity, today, is like an orphan crying in the night, crying for the light. It is the light of understanding the nations need. Today, we have arrived at a stage where, alike nations and individuals, must learn to understand one another or perish. There is no other choice!

The
Magic
Of
Forgiveness

The person who holds on to anger or resentment is, without his knowing it, causing damage to himself from within.

The person who forgives enters a new life of gentle peacefulness.

Forgiveness is its own reward. It is the forgiver rather than the forgiven who receives the greater benefit.

Forgiveness acts like magic. Forgiveness provides a magical solution to many of our problems.

CHAPTER ONE

Anger Ceaseth Not By Anger*

In the course of a debate in the American Congress, a senator, J. P. Benjamin, made a personal attack on senator W. H. Seward. It lasted for a considerable time. Then Benjamin resumed his seat, angry and bitter, to await a counter-attack.

To the wonder of all present, Senator Seward went over to his opponent and said sweetly:— "Benjamin, give me a cigar. When your speech has been printed, send me two copies."

Later, Seward was seen joking with his colleagues, puffing contentedly on the cigar he had received from his opponent.

Anger ceaseth not by anger, anger ceaseth by forgiveness. Forgiveness is, perhaps, the most powerful antidote to anger. Forgiveness and the willingness to be reconciled to those who, for some reason or the other, are not well–disposed towards us. Willingness to be reconciled is all that is needed. For, reconciliation is a two-way process into which a person cannot be forced. I can forgive another but cannot compel the other to forgive me in return.

Forgiveness has been defined as "a process of ceasing to feel resentment against someone or to pardon someone." To cling to resentments is to harm oneself, is to walk the way of spiritual death. To choose to let go of resentments is to walk the way that leads to a life of freedom and fulfilment. The person who

---

* Notes of a talk

57

holds on to anger or resentment is, without his knowing it, causing damage to himself from within. The person who forgives enters a new life of gentle peacefulness. Forgiveness is its own reward. It is the forgiver rather than the forgiven who receives the greater benefit.

Forgiveness acts like magic. Forgiveness provides a magical solution to many of our problems.

Man grows in true greatness in the measure in which he is able to express the quality of forgiveness. All our great ones have been men and women of forgiveness. Even so, forgiveness is not the monopoly of the great. Simple souls, humble men and women have practised the art of forgiveness to perfection.

A house, in which a man and his ten-year-old daughter lived, was attacked by some outlaws. The father died in the scuffle. The outlaws spared the life of the girl, Melania, but gouged out her eyes, so that she became blind. Ten years later, Melania was sitting by the roadside, when she heard footsteps and a voice which frightened her. "Who is it?" she called out, "Be careful, because I am blind."

"I know you are," replied one of the outlaws. "I am the man who killed your father and blinded you. I just tried to hold up a passer-by and he shot me. I am going to die. Pray forgive me."

Melania shuddered with anger but controlled herself, forgave the criminal and exhorted him to repent. When the man was dead, she groped for his eyes and gently closed them like a loving daughter.

The French Dauphin, son of Louis XVI, was a prisoner in the hands of a rough jailor, who treated him cruelly, for the crime of having been born as the son of a king.

One day, the jailor asked him:— "What would you do with me if the throne was restored to you and you become the King of France? Would you have me hanged?"

The orphan prince simply answered:— "I would forgive you!"

It is difficult to imagine what life would be without the spirit of forgiveness. How true it is that, he who has not forgiven an enemy, has never yet tasted one of the most sublime enjoyments of life. Let us forgive one another while there is yet time: for the day cometh when the opportunity to forgive will be taken away from us.

We are told that two of the greatest writers of the nineteenth century, Thackeray and Dickens, became rivals and estranged. Just before Christmas, 1883, they met in London and deliberately failed to recognise each other. Then suddenly, Thackeray turned back, seized the hand of Dickens and said he could no longer bear the coldness that existed between them. Dickens was touched: they parted with smiles. The old jealousy was destroyed.

Almost immediately afterward, Thackeray suddenly died. What a relief it must have been to Dickens that they had shaken hands so warmly a day or so before! We must not delay in seeking— or offering— forgiveness. For another opportunity may not be given us to do so.

CHAPTER TWO

Forget What God Hath Forgotten

As we grow spiritually, forgiveness becomes our second nature. We forgive even before forgiveness is asked. It is only then that we are filled with the peace that passeth, surpasseth understanding.

Forgiveness has a transforming power. They brought to Sadhu Vaswani a girl who had gone astray. Her eyes glistened with tears of repentance. Sadhu Vaswani said to her:— "Come near, my child."

The girl drew closer. Her tears dropped on Sadhu Vaswani's feet. Taking out his handkerchief, Sadhu Vaswani wiped the tears of the girl and said:— "My child, forget what God hath forgotten. Go and sin no more!"

The girl's life was transformed. This is the magic of forgiveness.

An editor of a newspaper, bribed by some wealthy people of the town, wrote untruths concerning Sadhu Vaswani and his noble work. Free copies of the newspaper were distributed in many homes.

Sometime later, the wife of the editor contracted tuberculosis. He desired to give her the best medical treatment but was short of money. When Sadhu Vaswani learnt of it, he passed on a bundle of notes to the editor and said:— "Brother, here is a little amount for your wife's treatment. If, at anytime, you need more, kindly let me know."

The editor's heart was touched. He became an ardent devotee and, till the last day of his life, attended Sadhu Vaswani's evening *satsang* (spiritual fellowship meetings). Such is the magic of forgiveness.

To err is human, to forgive divine. The more you learn to forgive, the more Godlike you become. God is the Ever–Free. The "f" of forgiveness is freedom. Forgiveness sets us free from the hurts which otherwise would continue to prick us for as long as memory lasts.

Within us there is the conflict between love and hate. Love asks to forgive, hatred seeks to get even, to return evil for evil. Has someone hurt me, cheated me, betrayed my trust, exploited me, spread scandals against me? Love tells me to forgive: hatred cries to get even, to take an eye for an eye, to give a blow for a blow. In the struggle, if love triumphs, I easily forgive the wrong-doer. If hatred has the upper hand, the memory of wrong done to me keeps on burning within me.

Several years ago, a man met me. His face was dark as charcoal. He said to me:— "There is a fire burning within me, and its flames will not be quenched until I have shot down the man who was indirectly responsible for the death of my father!" Yes—hatred is a fire that keeps on burning within you. It burns away your peace and happiness.

On the other hand, think of Mahatma Gandhi. He was nearly slain by a fanatic, in 1908, when he was in South Africa. Mahatma Gandhi said to his friends:— "This man did not know what he was doing. I will love him and win his love!" A year later, the man who wished to kill him, wrote to Mahatma Gandhi, offering his apologies and admiration. This is the magic of forgiveness.

There is a similar incident in the life of Pope John Paul. A man named Muhamad Ali tried to kill him in 1984. The Pope went to the Rabibbia Prison in Rome to meet the man. The Pope took the hand of the man who had fired a bullet at his heart, and forgave him.

Sadhu Vaswani, Mahatma Gandhi and the Pope were great men committed to the ideal of forgiveness. Let me give you an incident which occurred in the life of an ordinary man. He found a boy-thief in his flower garden. Quietly, he came up behind him, caught the boy by his shoulder and said to him:— "My boy, tell me which is the best flower in the garden?"

The boy, finding it impossible to escape, looked around and said:— "That rose is the best."

The man, still holding the boy by his shoulder,

plucked the rose in all its beauty and handed it over to the boy.

Amazed, the boy asked:— "Aren't you going to punish me?"

"No," said the man. "I am not going to punish you. But I am going to trust you that you will never steal from my flower-beds again, will you?"

"Never, Sir, as long as I live," was the emphatic reply. "But please, Sir, tell me if there is any little thing that I can do for you. I would wish to serve you as long as I live!"

There is the magic of forgiveness. Forgiveness and a token of love had won the hardened heart of the boy and he became a willing servant of the rich man.

CHAPTER THREE

Witness Of The Great Ones

We are under the influence of the unforgiving ego. It clamours for an eye for an eye, a tooth for a tooth. The ego does not want to forgive. In the measure in which we are released from the tentacles of ego, in that measure we grow in the quality of forgiveness.

Forgiveness has been an essential element in the lives of all the great ones of humanity. Think of Jesus. He harmed no one: he hurt no one. Yet, they captured him, at night, and held a mock trial and sentenced him to be crucified. From the Cross, Jesus looked at his captors and prayed:— "Father, forgive them, for they know not what they do!"

Sant Eknath was a picture of patience. He was always calm, unruffled, serene. Some of the wealthy people in the town were jealous of him: they hired a man and promised to reward him richly, if only he could make the Saint lose his temper.

Everyday, in the dark of the dawn, the Saint took a dip in the waters of the river. One day, as he returned to his cottage, after his morning bath, the hireling spat in his face. Quietly, the Saint went back to the river and had a second dip. Once again, as he was on his way home, the man spat at him. This unholy act was repeated for as many as 107 times. The Saint's patience was not tired. He went to the river and, for the 108th time, had a dip in the sacred waters. This time the heart of the hireling was touched. As the Saint wended his way homeward, the man fell at his feet and implored forgiveness:— "Forgive me, O Saint of God! I have greatly sinned!" The man explained that he had been bribed by some of the wealthy people to make the Saint lose his temper. The temptation of the reward made him behave so nastily.

"Forgive you, for what?" exclaimed the Saint. "Today, has been a unique day in my life: I have had 108 dips in the sacred waters. For this, I feel grateful." The Saint added:— "If only you had told me of the reward, I would have pretended to be angry, so that you could have claimed your reward!"

Think of Guru Amardas! He succeeded Guru Angad. Guru Angad's son, Datu, was disappointed. He felt it was his right to occupy the *Guru-gadi* (the seat of the Master). Full of anger, he came to Guru Amardas and said:— "Till yesterday, you were but a servant in our home. Today, you have occupied the *Guru-gadi!*" So saying, he kicked the aged Guru.

The Guru looked at him with compassionate eyes and said:— "I am an old man and my bones are hard. They must have hurt your foot. Forgive me!"

Such is the witness of the holy ones, the Saints of God, who have appeared in all climes and in all countries.

Think of Rishi Dayanand, the illustrious founder of the Arya Samaj. He was known for his fearlessness and frankness. He spoke the truth without fear or favour and, in the process, won the displeasure of many influential people. Some of them bribed his cook, Jagannath, to administer slow poison in his food.

Rishi Dayanand became seriously ill. The doctors realised that the great leader had been poisoned and there was no hope of recovery. When Rishi Dayanand learnt of it, he called Jagannath and, giving him some money, said:— "Escape to Nepal. Flee, while there is time. If my disciples learn of what has happened, they will kill you!"

Every great man has borne witness to the noble ideal of forgiveness.

Think of St. Teresa, the little flower. She lived in a convent— a life of goodness and purity and service, and this aroused jealousy among the other sisters. Some took advantage of her goodness. This is a common complaint. People say to me, you speak of the spirit of forgiveness. But if we continue to forgive, people take undue advantage. Teresa did not mind. She went a step further. She rejoiced when some of the other inmates of the convent took advantage of her.

She went on being humiliated, laughed at, chaffed. Some misunderstood her innocence and characterised it as stupidity: she did not mind. She went her way: she called it the "little way". She realised that until she had become nothing, until she had completely emptied herself, she would not be acceptable to the Lord. She understood that the key— the only key— to the portal of 'Being' is 'not-to-be.'

She wished to keep her cell clean and tidy. In her absence, some threw dirt and dust in the cell and made it unclean. She accepted it as God's Will: and never did a word of complaint leave her lips.

She was fond of a pretty little jug. Someone took it away. The pretty jug was replaced by a heavy, cracked one. "So much the better," she said to herself, "I will be free from attachment to things."

One evening, she could not find her lamp and had to go without her reading. She sat in the dark and experienced the joy of having absolutely nothing.

When she did anything for anybody, she hated to be noticed. She willingly accepted the blame that was due to others. She never tried to explain to her superior that someone else was the culprit. When she was wrongly blamed for having broken a vase, she kissed the ground and promised to be more careful. She went out of her way to do things for a sister who was rude to her: Teresa persevered with tireless patience until the cross-grained sister became a devoted and gentle friend.

She forgave the hurts she did not deserve and, in her heart, there was nothing but love for those who regarded themselves as her enemies but whom she thought of as children of God. She walked the way of forgiveness and became a Saint. Today, she shines as a radiant star in the firmament of the world's spiritual leaders.

CHAPTER FOUR

Four Stages

To arrive at forgiveness, one has to pass through four stages.

The first is the stage of hurt. Someone has wronged me, done something mean to me. Someone has been unfair to me: and I cannot forget it. I feel hurt. The hurt keeps on poking within me. It is here that we must remember that it is not I who feels hurt, but the ego.

A woman met a holy man and confessed that she had resentment in her heart against a prominent member of the community.

The holy man said to her:— "Go to her immediately. Don't try to justify or excuse yourself. Tell her that you have had unkind thoughts about her. Be humble and ask for forgiveness."

The woman said:— "I can't do that. I can't forget the hurt she had inflicted on me."

The woman was at the first stage—the stage of hurt. Those that are at this stage naturally hold grudges, not realising that the person who holds a grudge injures himself more than the one against whom the grudge is held.

Hatred and malice, like anger and worry, bring harm to the body, since they poison the blood. And they keep on increasing for "a grudge is the only thing that does not get better when it is nursed."

Hurt leads to hate which is the second stage. I

cannot forget how much I have been hurt and I cannot send out thoughts of good-will to my enemy. In some cases, I hate the person so much that I want him or her to suffer, as much as I am suffering.

Madam Chiang Kai Shek, we read, hated the Japanese. Her mother was a pious woman who prayed often. Madam Chiang Kai Shek said to her:— "Why don't you pray to God that He may drown Japan in the waters of the ocean?"

Her mother, of course, said to her:— "My child, how can I offer such an evil prayer?"

Hatred was painted by an artist as an old man shrivelled up and pale as death, clutching in his claws lighted torches and serpents, and cruelly tearing out his heart with black, decayed teeth.

Asked to explain the significance of the picture, the artist said:— "Hatred is an old man because it is as ancient as mankind, pale because he who hates, torments himself and lives a tragic life, with claws because it is so unmerciful, with torches and serpents because it creates discord, and it tears out its heart because it is self-destructive."

Hurt leads to hate. Then comes the third stage: it is the stage of healing. God's grace descends on me and I begin to see the person who has hurt me in a new light. I begin to understand his or her difficulty. My memory is healed and I am free again.

A girl came to a holy man and said:— "I know not why, but I am unable to sit in silence and pray or meditate. I feel restless: I used to be so happy."

The holy man asked:— "How is it?"

The girl answered:— "I think it has something to do with one whom, at one time, I regarded as a friend. But she was very cruel to me, and I said I would never forgive her, never talk to her. I am sorry I said it, but since then there has been no peace in my heart. What shall I do?"

The holy man said:— "It is better to break a bad vow than to keep it. Go to her and seek her forgiveness."

The next morning, she went to her friend and confessed her uncharitable attitude and asked her forgiveness.

The one whose forgiveness was sought burst into tears.

She said:—"You have come to ask for forgiveness. It is I who should be asking for forgiveness, for I am ashamed of my wrong attitude."

The two friends were reconciled.

Then comes the fourth stage: it is the stage of coming together. I am anxious to make friends with the person who hurt me, I invite him into my life. I share my love with him and we both move to a new and healed relationship.

When Abraham Lincoln was a young, struggling lawyer, he was employed on an important case. The fee was large. He travelled to a distant city for consultation with other lawyers on the case. One of them was Edwin M. Stanton. When he saw Lincoln sitting in the reception room, he said;— "What is he doing here? Get rid of him. I will not be associated with such a gawky ape as that!"

Lincoln pretended not to hear. In spite of the insult, he met the group of lawyers and went with them into the courthouse. As the trial proceeded, Lincoln was completely ignored. He was not even invited to sit with the other lawyers.

Edwin Stanton brilliantly defended his client. His arguments were masterful. His handling of the case held Lincoln spellbound. He won the case. That night, Lincoln said:— "His argument was a revelation to me. I have never heard anything so finished and so carefully prepared. I can't hold a candle to him. I'm going home to study law all over again."

Years passed. Lincoln became the President of

the United States. Among his most outspoken critics was Stanton who had cruelly insulted him and sorely wounded him. But Lincoln never forgot that Stanton was a man with a brilliant mind. When the time came to select a man to hold the vital post of Secretary of War, he chose Stanton. Only a man of Lincoln's magnanimity and forgiving spirit could have risen above Stanton's insult.

The day came when Lincoln lay dying— the victim of an assassin's bullet. When Lincoln's eyes finally closed in death, Stanton, disconsolate with grief, paid him a glowing tribute and said:— "Now he belongs to the ages!"

CHAPTER FIVE

10 Practical Suggestions

Now a few practical suggestions on how to walk the way of forgiveness. I call them the ten fingers of forgiveness.

PRACTICAL SUGGESTION NO. 1

When anyone hurts you immediately offer a prayer to God:— "O God, help me to forget this hurt, so that it does not enter my heart, and become a festering wound."

PRACTICAL SUGGESTION NO. 2

If anyone has hurt you to a point where you are unable to forget it— the memory of the

hurt keeps coming, again and again, and disturbs the peace of your mind— unburden yourself to a spiritual elder, or write a letter to the person against whom you hold a grudge.

Unburden yourself in the letter. Pour into it all the venom that is within you. Write as many harsh words as you possibly can. After you have done so, tear the letter into pieces and, as you keep on tearing the letter, breathe out a prayer that God's benedictions may flow into the life of the wrong- doer.

A man came to Abraham Lincoln and complained that someone had acted horribly towards him and he could not forget the hurt.

Lincoln said:— "Why don't you write to him a letter, telling him everything that you hold in your mind against him? Write as hard as you can."

The man went and wrote a very harsh letter, then came to Lincoln and said:— "I have written the letter as you advised. May I now post it to him?"

"Of course not," said Lincoln. "Now you tear it up and throw the pieces into the fire— and forget all about it!"

It becomes easier to forget when one has unburdened one's mind.

PRACTICAL SUGGESTION NO. 3

Forgive others but, also, forgive yourself!

Many of us carry on our hearts, heavy loads of guilt which rob us of our peace of mind. No man is perfect. Everyone of us has done some wrongs in the past— near or remote. We must repent and, if possible, make amends. We must pray for wisdom and strength not to repeat the wrong and then forget about it.

A husband told me that he and his wife had lived very happily for over fifteen years. Suddenly, something— he knew not what— happened and the wife became aloof, sad and depressed. At times, he would find her sitting in a silent corner, shedding tears. This, he said, had spoilt the atmosphere of the house. He had talked to his wife, but there was no response.

I met the wife privately and understood that she carried a guilt feeling on her mind. I told her that God is the great forgiver. He forgives: we must learn to accept His forgiveness and feel that we are forgiven. We must forgive ourselves!

She is a devotee of Sri Krishna. I said to her:— "When you find that you are alone in the house, go and sit at the Lotus Feet of Lord Krishna and actually describe to Him all that had happened. It will not do merely to tell Him:— "Lord, you are the all-knowing One and already know whatever has happened." Actually recount, in detail, the things which you feel you should not have done, then ask for forgiveness— and then, what is very important, forget all about it."

"Will Sri Krishna forgive me all that I have done?" she asked.

I said to her:— "Krishna forgives sins: by His power, sins are taken away and we can be free!"

That is the promise of Sri Krishna. Does He not say in the *Bhagavad Gita*:— "Come unto Me for single refuge, and I shall liberate you from all bondage to sin and suffering. Of this have no doubt!"

She did as she was told. After some days, the couple met me again, and I rejoiced to find a radiant smile on the face of the wife. She said to me:— "It is gone! It is gone!"

PRACTICAL SUGGESTION NO. 4

Never hold resentments against anyone, in the heart within.

If I hold a resentment against someone, I may not harm that person but will surely harm myself. Many suffer from bodily disease because of the grudges they hold in their minds against people.

A woman suffered from severe rheumatic pains in the knee joint. No medicines were of any avail. The pain went on increasing, until a holy man asked her:— "Do you hold a grudge against anyone?"

She hesitated, then answered:— "My mind is seething with resentment against my own sister who did not behave properly towards me."

The holy man said to her:— "Your pains will disappear only when you forgive her and make peace with her."

At first, she found it difficult to do so. Later, she met her sister and gave her a hug and said to her:— "Let bygones be bygones! Let us begin anew!"

To her amazement, she found that soon thereafter the pains disappeared.

PRACTICAL SUGGESTION NO. 5

Every night, as you retire, think of all the people who have hurt or wronged you, during the day. Actually, call their names and say:— "Mr. X, I forgive you! Mrs. Y, I forgive you! Miss Z, I forgive you! So help me God!"

You will have sound sleep at night, and the quality of your dreams will improve.

A barrister complained to a holy man that he could not get sleep at night. Oftentimes, he was awake, pacing up and down, in his room.

The holy man said:— "Tonight, before you retire, forgive all those who have wronged you, actually calling out their names."

The barrister did as he was asked to do. He called each person's name and said:— "Mr. A, I forgive you! Mrs. B, I forgive you! Miss C, I forgive you! So help me God!"

The barrister said that that was the first night in several years that he could sleep soundly.

PRACTICAL SUGGESTION NO. 6

We must make forgiveness a habit.

We must not rest content by forgiving once or twice or thrice. We must keep on forgiving as often as we are wronged. God forgives us, again and again. Howsoever wayward or disobedient we become, He is never tired of forgiving us. He is patient until, at last, we return to Him.

A man met me in Indonesia. He spoke to me of one of his assistants who had reported against him six times to the Tax Authorities. Then, every time he came back and begged forgiveness. "I have reinstated him six times," he said. "How many times am I supposed to forgive such a man?"

I said to him:— "A similar question was asked of Jesus. How many times shall we forgive? Shall we forgive seven times? And Jesus said:— "Seventy times seven!" Jesus meant to say that we must forgive as often as forgiveness is asked.

PRACTICAL SUGGESTION NO. 7

We must move a step further. We should forgive even before forgiveness is asked.

It was Jesus who said:— "Unto him that smiteth thee on the one cheek, offer also the other!" He also said that if a man compelled you to walk with him for a mile, go with him an additional mile.

This teaching has great therapeutic value. Whosoever lives up to this teaching finds that his interior peace is never disturbed. And is not peace the solid foundation of health?

A Quaker had a quarrelsome, disagreeable neighbour whose cow often got into the Quaker's well-cultivated garden.

One morning, the Quaker drove the cow to his neighbour's home and said to him:— "Neighbour, I have driven thy cow home once more. If I find her in my garden again...."

Before the Quaker could finish the sentence, the neighbour said angrily:— "Suppose you do? What will you do?"

"Why," said the Quaker softly, "I'll drive her home to thee again!"

The cow didn't give the Quaker any more trouble.

PRACTICAL SUGGESTION NO. 8

When we forgive, we must also forget.

Someone has said, I can forgive but I cannot forget. That is only another way of saying, I will not forgive. True forgiveness is like a cancelled cheque— torn and burned up so that it can never be shown against one.

There were two old friends who met each other, one evening, after several years. They decided to have dinner together. They sat and they talked, recalling many experiences of earlier days. Finally, one of them realised it was three o'clock in the morning. They said, we must hurry home.

The next day, they met again and one said to the other:— "How did your wife take your coming in so late, last night?"

The man replied:— "I explained to her, she understood and it was perfectly alright. How did your wife react?"

The man answered:— "When I got home, my wife became historical."

The friend said:— "You mean hysterical?"

"No," said the man, "I mean historical. She brought up everything that happened in the last thirty years of our married life!"

We must not be historical. When we forgive, we must forget. A friend of Clara Barton, founder of the American Red Cross, once reminded her of some cruel thing that had been done to her, years ago. But Miss Barton seemed not to recall it.

"Don't you remember it?" her friend asked.

"No," came the reply, "I distinctly remember forgetting that."

A man was on his death-bed. He held a grudge against a friend who had dealt with him unfairly. Before dying, he wanted to tell him that he had forgiven him. When the friend arrived, the man embraced him and said:— "I am about to die. I forgive you for whatever has happened."

The friend felt relieved, and his eyes glistened with unbidden tears.

Before the friend left, the dying man said:— "I forgive you only if I die. If I recover I take back my words."

PRACTICAL SUGGESTION NO. 9

Speak kindly concerning the person against whom you hold a grudge.

In fact you must go out of your way to help him, to serve him. That is the way God's grace will descend on you.

George Washington and Peter Miller were schoolmates. One became President of the U. S. A., the other, a preacher. A man named Michael Wittman persecuted Peter Miller and troubled him in many ways.

Suddenly, Wittman was involved in a charge of treason and was sentenced to death.

Miller walked seventy miles to Philadelphia to see Washington, who asked, "Well, Peter, what can I do for you?"

"For the sake of our old acquaintance, George, I have come to beg the life of Wittman."

"No, Peter, ask for something else," said Washington. "This case is too black. I cannot give you the life of your friend."

"My friend!" exclaimed Miller. "He is the bitterest enemy any man ever had." And he described what he had suffered at the hands of Wittman for over twenty years.

As Washington heard the story of Peter's persecution, he said:— "Ah, then, Peter, this puts another aspect upon the matter. You are pleading for the life not of a friend but your bitterest enemy. Surely, this is not the work of man, it is something divine. I can refuse man, but I cannot refuse God. I will freely pardon your enemy."

An English officer walked through the battlefield with his servant. He noticed a wounded enemy soldier crying for water.

"Give the poor fellow a drink from my water-bottle," the officer said to the servant.

As the servant stooped down to give water to the thirsty soldier, he immediately fired at him.

"And now, Sir, what do I do?" asked the servant, stepping back.

The officer answered:— "Give him the water, all the same!"

PRACTICAL SUGGESTION NO. 10

Forget yourself and actually love the person who has wronged you!

There was a couple— Edith and Carl Taylor. They loved each other with no ordinary love. Though they were not rich in the wealth of the world, just because of the love her husband showered upon her, Edith regarded herself as the luckiest woman in the

76

town. She and Carl had been married 23 years, but it appeared as though they were newly married. Her heart still skipped a beat when Carl walked into the room. Carl, too, loved his wife. Whenever his work took him out of town, he would write to Edith a love-letter every night. He sent her small gifts from every place he visited.

In February 1950, the Government sent Carl to Okinawa for a few months to work in a new warehouse. (Carl worked in the Goverment Warehouse Department.) This time, there were no daily letters and no gifts. Each time Edith enquired why Carl had been away for so long, he would write that he would have to stay another month or two. A year passed, but Carl did not return. His letters became less frequent and more formal: love was missing.

Then, after weeks of silence, a letter came:— "Dear Edith, I wished there were a kinder way to tell you that I have applied to Mexico for a divorce. I want to marry a Japanese woman whom I love. Aiko is her name. She is a maid-of-all-work who has served me so well."

The first reaction was shock, then fury. Should she fight that quick paper-divorce? She hated her husband and that woman for having shattered her life. Hurt had led to hate: and hate burnt within her. But the grace of God descended on Edith. Soon she arrived at the third stage— that of healing. She tried not to judge her husband but to understand his situation. He was a lonely man: his heart was full of love. Aiko was a penniless girl. Under these circumstances, it was so easy for a man and woman to come together. And Carl had not done a shameful thing. He had chosen the way of divorce rather than take advantage of a young servant girl. Aiko was 19: Edith was 48. Edith wrote to Carl, asking him to keep in touch with her, to write to her, from time to time, giving her all the news.

One day, Carl wrote that he and Aiko were expecting a baby. She was born in 1951. She was named Marie. Then in 1953, another girl was born, Helen. Edith sent gifts to the little girls. Carl and Edith continued to write to each other.

Edith had no interest in life: she just existed. She worked in a factory and earned a livelihood. She hoped that Carl would some day come back to her.

One day, she got a letter that Carl was dying of lung cancer. Carl's last letters were full of fear—not for himself but for Aiko and the two little girls. What will become of them? His entire savings were spent on paying hospital bills. He would die a penniless man.

It cost Edith a tremendous effort to take the decision. She loved Carl. What was there she could not do for the sake of that love! She wrote to Carl that if Aiko was willing, she would adopt Marie and Helen as her children. Edith realised that it would be hard, at the age of 54, to be a mother of two little children. "I shall do it for the sake of Carl," she decided.

Carl died. Edith looked after Marie and Helen. It was a hard job. She worked harder to earn a little more to feed the two extra mouths. She became ill, but she kept working because she was afraid of losing a day's salary. At the factory, one day, she fainted. She was in the hospital two weeks with pneumonia. There, in the hospital bed, her thoughts went out to Aiko. How lonely she must feel with her daughters away from her. Her husband dead: her children in a foreign land. What must be Aiko's condition?

Edith took the final step on the path of forgiveness. The mother must come and be with the children. But there was the immigration problem. Aiko was a Japanese citizen. And the immigration quota had a waiting list many years long.

Edith wrote to an editor of a paper who described the situation in his newspaper. Petitions were started. A special bill speeded through the Congress and, in August 1957, Aiko was permitted to enter the States.

As the plane arrived at New York's International

Airport, Edith had a moment of fear. What if she should hate the woman who had taken Carl away from her. Aiko was the last passenger to leave the plane. She did not come down the stairs. She clutched the railing and stood there. Edith realised how panicky Aiko felt. Edith summoned up sufficient strength and called Aiko's name, and the girl rushed down the steps and into Edith's arms. In that brief moment, as they held each other, Edith prayed:— "God, help me to love this girl as if she were a part of Carl come home. I prayed for him to come back. Now he is in his two little daughters and in the gentle girl that he loved. Help me, God, to know that!"

I will close with the simple question:— My dear brothers and sisters, tell me, could you have loved as much as Edith loved?

Before Edith died, she repeated the words she used to utter when she and Carl lived together:— "I am the luckiest woman in the town!"

This is the magic of forgiveness.

The Therapy Of Cheerfulness

Our blood molecules contain receptors which receive signals from the brain.

If a person is happy and contented, the receptors transmit the signals of happiness, and the healing process is accelerated.

This is a discovery of modern science:— As you laugh more, you grow more healthy.

CHAPTER ONE

Therapeutic Value Of Laughter*

Laughter is at once a physical, mental, spiritual tonic. So let us begin this evening's talk on "The Therapy of Cheerfulness" by giving a good, hearty laugh.

There was a town in which they wished to build a temple with a school attached to it and a dispensary where the poor would receive free medical aid. The entire project was estimated to cost a crore of rupees. Members of the fund-raising committee approached a rich *sethia* for a donation. The *sethia* was parsimonious by nature. They said to him:— "We want you to be the first to contribute to the Temple project. God has blessed you with rich abundance. Give us at least 1% of the total estimated cost of the project."

"How much would that be?" asked the *sethia*.

"The entire project is estimated to cost a crore of rupees," they explained to him. "1% would work out to a lac of rupees."

Immediately, the *sethia* took out his cheque-book and wrote out a cheque for Rs. 1,00,000/- and, handing it over to them, moved out of the house.

The members were taken aback. They were not ready for this quick response. They thought that if they asked for a lac of rupees, they would receive Rs.10,000/-.

Suddenly, one of the members discovered that the cheque was not signed.

---

* Notes of a talk

They rushed to the *sethia* and said to him:— "Sir, by mistake, you have forgotten to sign the cheque."

"It is not a mistake," said the *sethia*. "The Scriptures teach that donations to charitable causes should be anonymous. Let my donation, too, be anonymous."

There are many therapies, many pathies. They include allopathy, homoeopathy, chromopathy, naturopathy. There is the ayurvedic system of medicine. There is yogic therapy. There is also the therapy of cheerfulness— the therapy that tells us that if only we are cheerful and happy all the time, we should not fall ill, and if we do, we should recover rapidly.

There is a man who is 70 years old. He claims that there has not been a single day when he has fallen sick. Not once has he visited a doctor's clinic. The secret of his health he attributes to cheerfulness.

Some of you may have read Norman Cousins' *Anatomy of an Illness*. The book gives the fascinating story of how the author "laughed his way" to health out of a progressive, crippling illness that the doctors believed was incurable.

Norman Cousins, the American journalist, went to the U.S.S.R. in August 1964, on an official visit. He developed fever. The temperature kept rising. He flew back to the U. S. A. His fever and pains all over the body worsened and, within a few days, he was hospitalised, almost unable to move his limbs. The doctors diagnosed the disease as "Collagen", a systematic disease of the body's connective tissue. The doctors frankly said that his chances of living through it were one in five hundred: the recovery would require a miracle.

Norman Cousins, a brave soul who would not easily give in, reasoned with himself. He argued that if a person works under stress, worries much, lives in anxiety and fear, he suffers a breakdown in his health.

Therefore, the converse must be true. If a man is cheerful all the time, if there is love, faith, hope within him, he should overcome illness. If stress, anxiety, fear, worry pull a man down, faith, hope, love, laughter should pick him up.

He decided to be his own doctor and started seeing comic movies. He read jokes. He laughed, again and again. He laughed as often as he could. To his astonishment, he found he could give up his drugs. Within a few months, he was fit enough to play on the golf course and resume his journalistic work. The doctors were amazed.

In his book, Norman Cousins speaks of the life-force that is within each one of us. Indeed, the life-force is there within every cell of the human body. The Rishis of ancient India studied it in detail. They called it *prana*. The *pranic* energy is that which supports life. *Prana* is the energy of the universe. Mind is the instrument for using as well as wasting this precious energy. Not many of us, in our daily life, pay heed to the *pranic shakti*. The *prana* is perhaps, the least understood and the most unused power on earth.

When the book, *Anatomy of an Illness*, was first published, it created a stir in the medical circle. Today, doctors all over the world are beginning to realise the therapeutic value of cheerfulness. Many conferences and seminars have been held to assess the therapeutic value of laughter. Laughter has been called "internal jogging".

CHAPTER TWO

Laugh Your Way To Health!

The story is told of a man who, when a child of two, lost his eyesight. For almost thirty years, he lived in utter darkness. He was denied the joy of beholding the beauties of nature— the bubbling brooks, the swaying of trees, the richness of many–hued flowers, the splendour of the morning sun and the serenity of the sunset. At the age of 32, he had a cornea transplant which gave sight to his unseeing eyes. Suddenly, he found himself in a new world of beauty and radiance.

"What are your immediate reactions, now that you are able to see?" He was asked.

"So long as I dwelt in darkness, I always imagined that the faces of most men around me were bright, cheerful, gay. Now that I am able to look around, I am shocked to find that most faces are sad and glum. Scarcely do my eyes behold a cheerful, smiling countenance. Children, I find, are happy and bubbling with joy. But when they grow up, their smiles disappear, their joy evaporates."

Today, many doctors are of the view that if a man is happy and light-hearted, cheerful and contented, positive and uncomplaining, disease will not draw close to him and, even if it does , it will not stay with him for long.

"Laughter," says Dr. Wilde, "provides a rhythmic movement of the abdominal muscles, gently massages the intestinal organs, improves digestion and blood circulation."

At the Harvard and Yale Universities of America and at the UCLA's Neuropsychiatric Institute at West Los Angeles and at several other research institutions, neurobiologists and medical researchers have confirmed that smiling, laughing and cheerful expressions set in motion happy waves in the mind stuff and generate neuropeptides which revitalise the immunity system to prevent and fight disease. People who are free from jealousy, envy, greed, are more healthy than people who lead cloistered, unhappy lives.

New clinches and prescriptions given by modern physicians are being displayed in hospitals and clinics. "Laugh your way to health"; "Laughter may be hazardous to your illness"; "Cheerfulness is the new Wonder Drug" are some of them.

CHAPTER THREE

Medical Evidence

Doctors are of the view that our blood molecules contain receptors which receive signals from the brain. If a person is happy and contented, the receptors transmit the signals of happiness, and the healing process is accelerated. This is a discovery of modern science: as you laugh more, you grow more healthy. Jolly physicians, it is said, are better than pills.

Cheerfulness, it is believed, is the greatest lubricant of the wheels of life. It diminishes pain, fights disease, mitigates misfortunes, lightens burdens and eases one's life.

Laughter begins in the lungs and diaphragm, setting the liver, the stomach and other internal organs into quick jelly-like vibrations, which give a pleasant sensation and exercise almost equal to that of riding on horse back.

Even the deepest breathing will not ventilate the lungs so thoroughly as a few seconds of hearty laughter. The total capacity of the average pair of lungs is about 3,500 cubic centimetres, or ten times as much as is taken in with breathing. Hearty laughter makes us tingle with vitality because the increased amount of air taken into the lungs helps to refresh— or oxidise— the blood. The entire body— including the brain— is exposed to an increased amount of oxygen. It pays to laugh long and hard.

Listen to the words of Dr. Green:— "There is not one remotest corner or little inlet of the minute blood vessels of the human body that does not feel some wavelet from the convulsions occasioned by a hearty laugh!"

Dr. Annette Goodhart, a psychotherapist who teaches laughter therapy, says that her entire therapy is based on the premise:— "We don't laugh because we are happy: we are happy because we laugh."

At Yale University, experiments by Garry Schwartz and others have confirmed that by changing the muscle patterns of the face, one can alter inner moods. You can change your mood merely by looking at a mirror and broadening your face with a smile. Just smile and you can come out of a cloud of depression. We don't laugh merely because we are happy: we also become happy when we laugh.

Dr. Goodhart also tells us that the average expectation of an American woman's life is eight years longer than that of a man. What is the reason? She explains that the American society approves of giggling and laughter among girls and women, but denies this privilege to men. An American man is supposed to be serious and sober, not easily given to laughter.

When Swami Vivekananda visited America, during the close of the last century, he could not understand why clergymen wore solemn and serious faces and believed that it was irreligious to laugh in public. Swami Vivekananda was a child of joy: he was so spontaneous. He did not restrain himself from laughing at public meetings when the occasion demanded. The American clergymen did not approve of this conduct which they thought was "frivolous". Swami Vivekananda thundered at them:— "What business do you have with clouded faces? It is terrible. If you have clouded faces, do not go out that day, shut yourself up in your room. What right have you to carry this disease out into the world?"

One recalls the admonition of St. Francis of Assisi to his disciples:— "You must not behave outwardly like melancholy hypocrites. You must go about wearing smiling, fresh, gay, agreeable faces." Therefore, you must learn to laugh, again and again.

How I wished we had at our Hospital— the Sadhu Vaswani Mission's Inlaks and Budhrani Hospital— a laughing gallery where the patients could have comic films, humourous books and cartoons. We could have guest speakers who regale the patients with jokes and humourous stories.

I recall how, on the sacred Muharram Day, they took me to Imambara. There a wonderful man— Mr. Agha— met me. He said to me:— "Your friends of the Sadhu Vaswani Mission do a lot of service. They visit orphanages, homes for the handicapped, the aged, the blind, and look into their needs. I ,too, in my own humble way, render service to the people."

"What do you do?" I asked him.

"I appear on the T. V. and make the people laugh!"

How true it is that they, who make the people laugh, also serve. Many of us have forgotten the ancient art of laughing.

CHAPTER FOUR

Case Histories

Mr. Donald, a cancer patient, was hospitalised for many long days. Doctors despaired of his condition and gave him up as a lost case. Donald was taken to the UCLA's Neuropsychiatric Institute of West Los Angeles. He was kept in an atmosphere of cheerfulness and gaiety. An attempt was made to keep his spirits high. Stories, jokes, humourous and funny incidents were narrated to him. He was kept lively and jovial. This man, for whom the doctors said it would be difficult to live for more than two to three weeks, felt much better after six months and, after a year, was almost cured.

The example is given us of a young girl who was brought to a hospital suffering from the same dreaded disease. When she was being prepared to be taken to the operation theatre, she found the nurses sad and glum. "I know what you are thinking of," she said to them. "But, let me tell you, I am not going to die so soon. God has other plans for me. I have spoken to Him and that is what He has told me."

When she was taken to the operation theatre, she kidded the doctors, until she came under the influence of the anaesthetic. The doctors opened her up and found that cancer had spread so extensively that it was no use performing the operation. They immediately stitched her up.

When she regained consciousness, she was told that she has only three to six months to live. She was advised to restrict her movements and live a relaxed, activity-free life.

The young woman was not taken in. "I have long cherished a desire to visit Switzerland," she said. "And even if it takes the life out of me, I will do it! Switzerland is said to be a heaven on earth. Before I visit God's heaven, let me see the beauty of the earthly heaven so as to be able to compare the two and find out which is the better one."

Doctors did all they could to dissuade her. "The strain of the trip to Switzerland will surely kill you," they warned her. However, when they found the woman adamant, they said to her:— "The climate of Switzerland and the change may do you good, though the strain of the travel may kill you."

Both the travel and the climate did her good. When she set out on the travel, she had to be taken in a wheelchair: when she returned, she walked with a straight gait, with a rose-tint on her cheeks. The doctors were amazed. Till this day she lives a happy life and bears testimony to the fact that if a person lives cheerfully, not focussing her attention on disease and illness, health and strength, vigour and vitality will belong to her.

Indeed, there would be no need of so many hospitals, if only people could be happy, light-hearted and gay!

CHAPTER FIVE

Does God Laugh?

Dr. Albert Schweitzer had his famous hospital in Equatorial Africa, where the climate is hot and humid. The doctors, who assisted him, came from Europe and felt quite uncomfortable and were often thrown out of their moods. Dr. Schweitzer made use of the therapy of cheerfulness on his medical staff. The therapy worked wonders on his young doctors and nurses, invigorating their sagging spirits and giving relief to their taut nerves. Everyone looked forward to meal times at which Dr. Schweitzer would relate to them amusing stories, humourous anecdotes and offer witty remarks.

All the great ones of humanity have been lovers of laughter. Socrates, St. Francis of Assisi, St. Teresa of Avilla, Sri Ramakrishna Parmahansa, Sri Ramana Maharishi, Papa Ramdas, Mahatma Gandhi and Sadhu Vaswani, to name but a few, all possessed a deep sense of humour.

Mahatma Gandhi said:— "If I didn't have my sense of humour, I would have committed suicide long ago."

Papa Ramdas said:— "I did not have to shed tears. I laughed my way to God."

Sadhu Vaswani had sparkling wit and humour, which would make us, at times, burst with laughter. One day, a doctor came to him and said:— "I have decided to give up my practice and devote all my time to the service of the country."

Sadhu Vaswani said to us:— "I am not sure if he is giving up his practice or if his practice is giving him up!"

A young man came to Sadhu Vaswani and said to him:— "You talk of God. But where is God? God is nowhere!"

Sadhu Vaswani asked the young man to write those words on a piece of paper. Sadhu Vaswani picked up a pencil and quietly drew a line between the "w" and "h" of nowhere, and asked the young man to read what was written. The young man read:— "God is now here!"

A man came to Sadhu Vaswani and said:— "I have served the people for a number of years. I want them to elect me to a seat in the Assembly."

Quietly, Sadhu Vaswani answered:— "The reward of service is more service!"

St. Francis of Assisi called his brother Friars in the Order "Jesters of the Lord".

St. Teresa of Avilla had a beautiful sense of humour. One day, she had walked quite a distance, and felt tired. Someone offered her an ass to ride. She rode a short distance when, suddenly, the ass collapsed and dropped down dead. She heard a Voice whisper in her ears:— "Teresa, this is how I treat my friends."

Immediately Teresa retorted:— "Lord, that is why you have so few friends!"

"Does God laugh?" I am asked.

Yes, God does laugh! He never laughs at our weaknesses and imperfections, our heartaches and headaches. But He does laugh at the ungodly world which thinks it can efface God out of existence. He laughs at our schools and colleges where, in the name of secularism, a godless education is given to our boys and girls, the "builders of tomorrow". God laughs when some of us remark that we can teach God how to make a better world. There is a wealthy woman who rejoices in saying:— "I wished God made me His secretary, I would teach Him how to make a better and happier world!"

I believe it was Sri Ramakrishna Parmahansa who said:— God laughs when a doctor assures his patient that if he takes his medicine, he will recover soon. God laughs, for He knows that the man is going to die that very night. God also laughs, when two brothers get together and draw a line and say, this property is mine and that is yours. God laughs, for He knows that all property belongs to mother earth.

CHAPTER SIX

Nine Practical Suggestions

I would wish to pass on to you a few practical suggestions on how a person can keep up the spirit of cheerfulness.

PRACTICAL SUGGESTION NO. 1

Get up in the morning with a smile on your face and the words, "Good morning, Lord!" on your lips.

Those words form the title of a book written by an American businessman. He says he gets up with those words on his lips, every morning. He has been doing so over a long period and claims that, by merely doing so, he has added a new dimension to his life.

PRACTICAL SUGGESTION NO. 2

See that your face always wears a smile.

It was Mahatma Gandhi who said:— "You are not completely dressed until your face wears a smile!" It has been said, wear a smile and you have friends: wear a scowl and you have wrinkles. Which would you have?

A smile is infectious. It is mirrored in the face of the one you smile at. Therefore, wherever you go, keep on smiling. Be careful to see that your smiles always announce sweetness and goodness, never betray sarcasm, bitterness or pride.

PRACTICAL SUGGESTION NO. 3

Give a hearty laugh at least three times everyday— once before breakfast, once before lunch, and once before dinner.

If you find it difficult to laugh, look into the mirror and make funny faces.

A family, I know, follows this principle. Before dinner, each member of the family tells something which makes the others laugh. Only then do all the members partake of their meals.

PRACTICAL SUGGESTION NO. 4

Develop a healthy sense of humour.

A sense of humour will save you from many difficult situations.

Two American senators got into an argument. One of them was tall and hefty, the other was short and slim. The former lost his temper and said:— "If I liked, I could swallow you up!"

The other answered with a smile:— "If you did

so, you would have more brains in your stomach than in your head!"

Two persons happened to pass through a passage in opposite directions. The passage was too narrow for both to pass at the same time. Where they met, one said rudely to the other:— "Make way for me!"

The other gently answered:— "I was about to say the same to you."

To which the first retorted:— "I never make way for a fool!"

The other quietly stepped aside and said:— "I do!"

Of Bernard Shaw, we are told, that a beautiful woman met him, one day, and said:— "You have the best intellect in the world and I have the most beautiful face. If we married, we would be able to produce the perfect child."

Bernard Shaw answered:— "Do you imagine what would be the child's condition if he had your brains and my face?"

There is another amusing incident told us concerning Bernard Shaw. He was tall and lean, while G. K. Chesterton was short and stout. When both came, face to face, Chesterton laughed and said:— "If people looked at you, they might think a famine has come to England."

"And if they looked at you," Shaw replied good humouredly, "they would know whom to blame!"

Mark Twain, the great humourist, once went to hear a lecture of a distinguished person. When the lecture was over, Mark Twain went up to the speaker and complimented him:— "Sir, your lecture was great. But, believe me, each word that you spoke is already written in a book."

The distinguished speaker, not having an adequate sense of humour, was naturally annoyed.

"Do you mean to say that I have memorized some

one else's lecture and reproduced it, word by word?" he angrily asked.

"I didn't mean to say that," replied Mark Twain mischievously.

"I would like to see that book," the speaker demanded.

"I shall soon send it to you!"

When the speaker got back, his mind was agitated. He could not rest in peace till the book had been brought to him. When finally the book arrived, he was pleasantly surprised to find that it was a dictionary!

PRACTICAL SUGGESTION NO. 5

Learn to laugh at yourself.

We often laugh at the oddities and weaknesses of others but not at our own. We must learn to laugh at ourselves.

It has been rightly said that the person who can laugh at himself is a delight to be with: he applies to his ills and errors the most soothing balm the human spirit has desired— laughter.

Bishop Fulton Sheen narrates, with a merry twinkle in his eyes, an incident from his life. One day, he visited a new place where he had to deliver a lecture at the Town Hall. He left the hotel early and decided to walk down to the Hall. Being a stranger to the city, he soon lost his way.

Approaching a group of little children, busy at play, he inquired:— "Could you please tell me the way to the Town Hall?

One boy stepped forward and gave him the directions and then asked:— "Why are you going to the Town Hall?"

"To give a lecture."

"On what?"

"On the Way to the Kingdom of Heaven!"

The child rippled with laughter and said:— "You do not know the way to the Town Hall. How can you tell the people the way to Heaven?"

Many of us think that we are the acme of perfection. But each one of us has so many oddities at which we can laugh.

The great sculptor, Daniel Chester, carved a statue of Emerson. Everyday, Emerson sat in front of the artist while he was at work. One day, looking at the statue, the sage of America exclaimed:— "The more it resembles me, the worse it appears!"

PRACTICAL SUGGESTION NO. 6

Always look at the bright side of things.

Everything has two sides— the bright and the dark or, as I would wish to put it, the bright and the less bright.

A king had a dream in which he found that all his teeth had fallen out. He wanted an interpretation of the dream. A dream interpreter was sent for. He consulted the ancient books and said to the king:— "Sire, this is a most unfortunate dream. It signifies that all your dear ones,— children, wife, relatives,— will die during your lifetime."

The king was disappointed and ordered that the soothsayer be thrown into prison.

Another dream interpreter was called for. He, too, consulted the same ancient books and said:— "O king, this is a most fortunate dream. It signifies that you will survive all your dear ones. Long live the king!"

The king felt happy and richly rewarded the soothsayer.

Both statements have the same meaning. But it is the way you put it or look at it that matters.

PRACTICAL SUGGESTION NO. 7

**Be sure that God is in charge of the
Universe. He is the controller of the
destinies of individuals and nations. And
nothing can ever go wrong.**

So many things happen to us, we are unable to
understand the "why" of them. Our dear ones are
suddenly snatched away from us. Misfortunes hit us.
Calamities befall us. Losses ruin us. If only we have
the faith that God is too loving to punish and too
wise to make a mistake, we shall not be upset. Faith
giveth courage. The man of courage will never
give up.

PRACTICAL SUGGESTION NO. 8

Be in the driver's seat all the time.

Don't let anyone else drive you. Be your own
master. There are so many people who do things to
you and you feel hurt and insulted. By doing so, you
merely let them drive you. You let them become your
masters.

George Washington Carver said:— "I will never
let anyone so degrade me that I hate him!"

PRACTICAL SUGGESTION NO. 9

**If you would be happy, make others happy.
The happiness that goes out of you to
others, comes back to you. Such is the law!
Therefore, do at least one good deed of
service everyday.**

A man met me and said:— "I am poor in the
wealth of the world and cannot give money and other
things to those in need. I simply cut out cartoons,

funny faces and jokes from newspapers and magazines and collect them in an album. Every evening, I carry the album to the children's ward of the Government Hospital. There I read out to the sick children something funny and show them cartoons and funny faces in the album. The little children, in the throes of suffering and pain, cannot help but laugh. As they look at the caricatures, they forget their suffering for a while, and their faces begin to smile. Some of them even laugh. Their eyes sparkle with delight as they temporarily forget their ailments. How they look forward to my daily visits!"

CHAPTER SEVEN

The Devil's Tool

There is a touching, little story told us of a Buddhist *bhikkhu*. He was the son of a nobleman and lived in a palace. Coming under the influence of the Buddha, he renounced his wealth and comfort and accepted the hardships of a mendicant's life. He slept on the bare ground: he ate what he got by way of alms. Suddenly, he got an attack of rheumatic pain. At first, he treated it with indifference. Days passed by: the pain persisted. He could not walk with ease. At times, he could not meditate properly. He felt miserable. Gone was the joy of his life. However hard he tried, he could not recapture the peace which once belonged to him.

One day, he found a little girl playing with her friends. She hobbled on sticks: but her face was a picture of joy. She was happy as a wave dancing on the sea. Seeing her, the *bhikkhu* felt ashamed of himself. "The little girl has only one leg and is bright and happy," he said to himself. "And I, a disciple of the Buddha, despair because of a little pain!"

Sadness is not due to what happens to us: it is due to what happens within us. Significant are the words of Oliver Cromwell, the man who must have faced dangers and difficulties almost everyday:— "I bless God I have been inured to difficulties and I never found God failing when I trusted in Him." If only we learnt to trust Him, in all situations and circumstances of life, no disappointment or depression would be able to touch us.

The man who has learnt the art of living draws, from the trials and tribulations of life, the strength he needs to serve God and His suffering creation. Difficulties, disappointments melt away before a man who has a cheerful disposition.

A significant story tells us of how the devil announced that he was going out of business and that he would sell his tools at a discounted price.

The tools were attractively displayed. They included self-love, egoism, sensuality, hatred, wrath, greed, envy, jealousy, passion for power, etc.

There was, however, one tool which appeared to be much worn out. The devil was not prepared to part with it except for an exceedingly exorbitant price.

Someone asked him:— "What is that?"

The devil answered:— "That is discouragement and depression."

"Why is it priced so high?"

"Because to me it has proved to be the most useful. When all other tools fail, I can, with this single tool, pry open the heart of man, and do my work. If only I succeed in making a man feel discouraged, disheartened, I can make him do what I like. I have used this tool almost on every man, that is why it is so much worn out."

It has truly been said that "the devil has two

master tricks." One is to get us discouraged: then, for some time at least, we can be of no service to others, and so are defeated. The other is to make us doubt, thus breaking the faith link by which we are bound to God. Look out! Do not be tricked either way!

Therefore, laugh and smile all the while! Laugh your way to health, happiness, harmony, prosperity and peace!

"Which is the most important of the five senses?" I was asked.

"None of them," I replied, "But the sixth one, the sense of humour."

Smile, Smile, All The While!

A
Question- Answer
Session with
Dada J. P. Vaswani

Let us fill our hearts with love,— love of God, love of our fellow human beings, love of brother birds and animals.

When our hearts are saturated with love, there will be no place in our life for unhappiness.

We shall be amongst the happiest of men on earth.

IF YOU HAVE NOTHING ELSE TO GIVE, GIVE A SMILE!

Question:— Dada, what is the thought for the day?

Dada :— The thought for the day is expressed in the words of Mahatma Gandhi:— "You are not completely dressed, until your face wears a smile."

Your dresses may be made of the best materials, they may have been stitched by the best dressmakers, but you are not completely dressed, until your face wears a smile.

Our Beloved Master, Sadhu Vaswani, said on one occasion:— "I have but one tongue. If I had a million tongues, with everyone of those million tongues I would still utter the one word:— Give! Give! Give!"

To give is to live! They that give live, they that give not are no better than dead souls!

Give, yes: give whatever you have; give of your time and talents, your wealth, your bank accounts, your experience, your wisdom, your knowledge. And if you have nothing else to give, you can give at least a smile. Until a stage comes when your face always wears a smile. Smile, smile, all the while!

A PERMANENT SMILE

Question:— There is always a smile on your face, and wherever you go, you spread the sunshine of joy and laughter. What is the secret, Dada?

Dada :— I do not know if there is always a smile on my face. Surely, there must be occasions when my face does not wear a smile. Yet this I know, that if a person lives and moves and does his daily work in the ever-living, the ever–loving, the ever-radiant, the ever-smiling presence of the Mother Divine, his face will continue to radiate a sweet, seraphic smile, all the time.

God is usually thought of as our Father, "our Father which art in Heaven". But God is both masculine and feminine. I often go to God, I approach God as the Mother Divine. Sitting at Her feet, gazing at Her face, I pray:— "Mother mine, make me Thine, make my life divine!" It is only when we grow in the life divine, the life that is life indeed— the life of communion and compassion, communion with the Highest, and compassion, which expresses itself in loving service of the lowliest and the least— that there appears spontaneously, on our face, a sweet, seraphic smile.

Such a smile is an expression of interior joy. Within us is a fount of joy and peace, the joy that no ending knows, the peace that passeth, surpasseth understanding. In the measure in which we unfold this joy, in that measure we will find a smile appears on our face automatically.

If the smile is forced, it will not last, it will fade away. The smile that comes from within is a permanent smile. Everyone of us carries that fount of joy and peace: everyone of us is, essentially, that peace, that joy. We are not the bodies with which we have identified ourselves. We are essentially That.

The *rishis* of ancient India referred to It as *Sat Chit Ananda*. *Sat* is usually translated as existence. I love to use the word abidingness, eternity. Everyone of us is eternal, deathless, immortal. Death cannot touch us, death can only touch the bodies that we wear. The body is a garment which we have worn during our period of earth existence. *Chit* is usually translated as consciousness. I love to use the word, awareness. *Ananda* is the joy, the endless joy that no one can take away from you, for it does not depend on outer conditions and things.

The great one who appeared, two thousand years ago, said:— "Nothing in the morn have I, and nothing

106

do I have at night, yet there is none on earth happier than I!"

This happiness is the birthright of everyone of us.

THE UNHAPPY MILLIONAIRE

Question:— Why is it that though the source of joy is within us, many of us are unhappy?

Dada:— How true it is that many of us are unhappy. It is not only the poor who are unhappy, but even the wealthy ones— millionaires and multi–millionaires— are unhappy. They have met me, a number of multi–millionaires and, with tears in their eyes, have said to me:— "We are unhappy, what shall we do?"

There is a multi–millionaire in London. He is a master of several millions of pounds sterling. In the course of a letter, he wrote:— "I have everything that the world can give. I am a master of pleasures and possessions and power. Yet there is not a day when I do not think of committing suicide."

SECRET OF HAPPINESS

Question:— We all wish to be happy: tell us if there is anything that we can do to make ourselves truly happy?

Dada:— I would wish to tackle this question first from a negative angle. We all wish to be happy. Yes, but there are very few who can truthfully say that they are truly happy. The reason is this, that we have not freed ourselves of all those things that keep a person unhappy. We cling to them as though they were the best of our friends. Let us cleanse our minds of all those things that destroy our happiness.

One of the destroyers is hate. There are so many who love hatred in their hearts. Hatred and happiness can never live together, even as light and darkness can never dwell together.

If someone hates me, I hate him in return. Hatred keeps on growing. Gautama Buddha said:— "Hatred ceaseth not by hatred, hatred ceaseth by love."

There was a man who was given to evil ways. He was a gambler and a drunkard. He visited houses of ill-fame. His wife, just to get a little solace and comfort, came to our Beloved Guru's (Sadhu Vaswani's) evening *satsang*. The husband did not approve of it and, one day, he came and shook his fist at Sadhu Vaswani and said:— "If only you knew how much I hate you!"

Sadhu Vaswani was the very picture of love, gentleness, humility. He looked lovingly into the eyes of the man and said:— "Brother, if only you knew how much I love you!"

The words worked a miracle. The man fell at the feet of Sadhu Vaswani and, with tears in his eyes, said:— "Forgive me, O saint of God, I have sinned greatly!"

His life was changed: he became a new man. From that day onwards, he, his wife and children regularly came to the evening *satsang*. How true it is that hatred ceaseth not by hatred, hatred ceaseth by love!

If you want to grow in happiness you must have love in your hearts. It is love that maketh a person happy.

HOW TO OVERCOME FEAR AND RESENTMENT

Question:— Dada, hatred surely is a destroyer of happiness. In our daily life, we feel upset over little things, trifles. Someone does not treat me in the right fashion, someone ignores me, someone speaks ill of me, and I feel easily upset. A feeling of resentment wakes up within me. Would you call that also a destroyer of happiness?

Dada:— Surely yes, resentment is a great destroyer

of happiness. Little things happen to us in our everyday life, and we feel irritated. Those little pricks of irritation distrub our happiness. The way out is to realise that whatever happens, happens according to the Will of God. And in the Will of God is the Highest Good of man.

Has anything happened to irritate you? Has anything happened which you did not want to happen? Realise that it has come to you out of the Loving Hands of God. Accept it as *prasadam* from the Lord, and you will never be irritated.

Yet another destroyer of happiness is fear. With fear in our hearts, we can never be happy. It was the great Vedic *rishi* who prayed:— "May I be free from fear of the friend and from fear of the foe! May I be free from fear of the known and from fear of the unknown!"

They asked Yudhishthira:— "What is it that rescues man from all types of danger?" His answer was in one word:— "Courage!"

Courage rescues us from all types of danger. Therefore, it is said:— When you lose wealth you lose little: when you lose a friend you lose much: but when you lose courage you lose your all!

Courage is born of faith— the faith that you are not alone. And faith is a gift of God. Therefore, we must pray, again and again, for faith.

BUILDING BLOCKS OF LIFE

Question:— Dada, in your talks you lay emphasis on right thinking. Could you tell us something about what part thought plays in our life?

Dada:— A very significant question. Usually, we pay scant attention to our thoughts. We say after all it was a thought, what does it matter? No, thoughts are forces. Thoughts are things. Thoughts are the building blocks of life. With our thoughts, we are building our future.

People usually blame their destiny. They say such is our fate, such are our stars. We forget that we are the builders of our own destiny. We are the creators of our own fate. We build our destiny with our thoughts. Every thought that we think is a brick with which we are building our destiny, our future. Therefore, we must always be careful of our thoughts.

A thought, when it is consistently held in the mind, drives a man to action. If it is a thought of service, it will lead to an act of service. If it is a thought of impurity, it will lead to an act of impurity. An action, repeatedly performed, forms a habit. And a habit is a terrible thing. Take away its "h", and "a bit" will remain. Take away the "a" and "bit" will still remain. Take away "b" and "it" will still remain.

The sum total of our habits forms our character. Character determines our destiny. The beginning is in the thought. Therefore, Benjamin Franklin said:— "The greatest discovery of our generation is that by changing your thoughts, you can alter your life."

There are so many people who, through their thoughts, draw to themselves calamities and misfortunes. Thought has magnetic power. We draw to ourselves that which we think of consistently and continuously.

Doctors today, speak of a new disease. They call it "symptomatic imaginities". A person has simple symptoms and he begins to imagine that he has contracted a dread disease. There is a woman, if ever she gets a headache, she begins to imagine that she has developed a tumour in the brain. There is a man, whenever he gets a stomach–ache, he feels he has developed cancer of the stomach. By imagining and thinking thus, we draw those diseases to ourselves. Therefore, we must be very careful about our thoughts.

THE MAN WHO WAS TRAPPED IN A
COAL-MINE

Question:— Dada, you said that you will first tackle the problem from a negative angle, what about the positive angle?

Dada:— The positive angle is this. If we want to be happy, we must fill our hearts with love,— love of God, love of our fellow human beings, love of brother birds and animals. When our hearts are saturated with love, there will be no place in our life for unhappiness. We shall be amongst the happiest of men on earth.

They asked Rabia, the great Muslim woman-saint:— "Don't you hate Satan?"

She answered:— "My heart is so full of love that there is no place in it for hate."

I read concerning a dying miner. He was trapped in a coal-mine and was about to pass away. He took a pencil and wrote on a small slip of paper his last letter to his wife:— "Do not worry about me, for I die a happy man. My love moves out to you, to the children and, above all, to God. He is by me, in this moment of danger. I can feel His presence with me. Therefore, am not afraid. My heart is filled with happiness. Give my love to the children. Take care of them. See that they grow to be men and women, fearless, full of courage, and full of the spirit of sympathy and service."

There was a man who knew what it was to love.